Modern Critical Interpretations

Stendhal's
The Red and the Black

Modern Critical Interpretations

These and other titles in preparation

Modern Critical Interpretations

Stendhal's
The Red and the Black

Edited and with an introduction by
Harold Bloom
Sterling Professor of the Humanities
Yale University

Chelsea House Publishers ◇ *1988*
NEW YORK ◇ NEW HAVEN ◇ PHILADELPHIA

© 1988 by Chelsea House Publishers, a division
of Chelsea House Educational Communications, Inc.,
  95 Madison Avenue, New York, NY 10016
  345 Whitney Avenue, New Haven, CT 06511
  5068B West Chester Pike, Edgemont, PA 19028

Introduction © 1988 by Harold Bloom

Printed and bound in the United States of America

∞ The paper used in this publication meets the minimum
requirements of the American National Standard for
Permanence of Paper for Printed Library Materials,
Z39.48-1984.

Library of Congress Cataloging-in-Publication Data

Stendhal's The Red and the black
   (Modern critical interpretations)
   Bibliography: p.
   Includes index.
   Summary: A collection of critical essays on Stendhal's novel
"The Red and the Black" arranged in chronological order of
publication.
   1. Stendhal, 1783–1842. Rouge et le noir. [1. Stendhal,
1783–1842. The red and the black. 2. French literature—
History and criticism] I. Bloom, Harold.   II. Series.
PQ2435.R72S78   1988   843'.7   87-9243
ISBN 1-55546-076-3 (alk. paper)

Contents

Editor's Note

This book brings together a representative selection of the best modern critical interpretations of Stendhal's novel *The Red and the Black*. The critical essays are reprinted here in the chronological order of their original publication. I am grateful to Suzanne Roos for her assistance in editing this volume.

My introduction argues that Stendhal is the Thomas Hobbes of Romantic novelists, more a materialist metaphysician of eros than he is a moral psychologist. René Girard, himself a metaphysician of novelistic eros, begins the chronological sequence with his celebrated analysis of how Stendhal perceived the comedy of mimetic or triangular desire, but not, according to Girard, its later tragedy.

The formalist mandarin Harry Levin gives us a very different *Red and the Black,* an original social vision in which Julien's hypocrisy, like Hamlet's madness, serves as a dramatic device. Refreshingly, D. A. Miller illuminates Julien's attempt to murder Mme de Rênal as a rescue expedition "to save what she has meant to him—to put her back in her place at the dead center of red." Peter Brooks, like D. A. Miller a critic who knows how difficult it is to *use* Freud, shrewdly traces what is most problematic in Julien's relation to the paternal principle. Stendhal's placement of the burden of representation upon his readership is highlighted in Ann Jefferson's account of *The Red and the Black*'s acute consciousness of the readers' share.

Margaret Mauldon, outlining the relation of *The Red and the Black* to the tradition of the epistolary novel, usefully concludes that Stendhal's great work is "a catalogue of miscommunications: of misleading roles assumed or imposed, of mistaken identities, of misunderstanding, misrepresentations and misreadings." In this book's final essay, Carol A. Mossman surveys the interlocking patterns of Julien's and Mathilde's separate "novels," until the two converge upon the final image of Julien's severed head.

Introduction

Nietzsche saluted Stendhal as "this strange Epicurean and man of interrogation, the last great psychologist of France." Yet Stendhal is both less and more than a psychologist, even in the sense of moral psychologist intended by Nietzsche. If we are unhappy because we are vain, which seems true enough, then the insight seems related to the conviction that our sorrows come to us because we are restless, and cannot sit at our desks. To assimilate Stendhal to Pascal would be tasteless, yet to determine the pragmatic difference between them is a complex labor. Pascal, to me, is the authentic nihilist; Stendhal is something else. Call that Julien Sorel, who attracts us without compelling our liking. Or do we like him? Robert M. Adams coolly concludes that:

> Whether you like Julien Sorel, and for what parts of his behavior, depends, then, in some measure, on who you think you are and what conspiracies or complicities your imagination allows you to join, in the course of reading the book.

That may be giving Stendhal the best of it, since the reader's fundamental right, as critic, is to ask the writer "who do you think you are, anyway?" The reversal is shrewd, whether Stendhal's or Adams's, since we do not expect the author to be quite as aggressive as ourselves. Stendhal brazenly excels us, and Julien is more his surrogate than many have allowed. We admire Julien for the range of his imagination, and are a little estranged by his extraordinary (if intermittent) ability to switch his affections by acts of will. He is, of course, designedly a little Napoleon, and if one is not Hazlitt or Stendhal that may not move one to affection. But the Napoleonic is only one wave or movement in him, and Stendhal is one of that myriad of nineteenth-century writers of genius who fracture the self. A more crucial movement is the Byronic, and here Adams is very perceptive indeed, marvelously so:

Most of what we think about Julien depends, of course, on our judgment of his behavior with the two ladies; and here we come up against the central paradox of the novel, that (like the ladies) we don't really think more highly of our hero the better he behaves. Quite the contrary. The worse he behaves, the more painful the sacrifices he requires of them, the more we are impressed by their determination to love him. Impervious to jealousy, untouched by his effort to murder her, Mme. de Rênal defies public scandal, leaves her husband and children, and comes to be with Julien in the hour of his anguish. Mathilde is in despair that he no longer loves her though she has sacrificed even more prodigally to her love of him. The revelation of Julien is not to be made directly, in the glare of open daylight, but only through the glow reflected on the faces of these devoted acolytes. As with Christ and Dionysus, the mystery of Julien is performed in the darkness of a prison-tomb, and his resurrection is celebrated in the presence of women. The cenacle of Julien allures its converts by withdrawing its mystery, etherealizing its cult: that is the work of the book's last important section.

One could argue that Julien, like Lord Byron, has that cool passivity which provokes his women into a return to themselves, so that his function is to spur these remarkable (and very dissimilar) ladies on to the epiphanies of their own modes of heroism. This could account for what I myself find most unsatisfactory about *The Red and the Black,* which is the obscurity (perhaps even obscuratism?) of Julien's final state of the soul:

The bad air of the prison cell was becoming insupportable to Julien. Fortunately on the day set for his execution a bright sun was shining upon the earth, and Julien was in the vein of courage. To walk in the open air was for him a delicious experience, as treading the solid ground is for a sailor who has been long at sea. There now, things are going very well, he told himself, I shall have no lack of courage.

Never had that head been so poetic as at the moment when it was about to fall. The sweetest moments he had ever known in the woods at Vergy came crowding back into his mind, and with immense vividness.

Everything proceeded simply, decently, and without the slightest affectation on his part.

Two days before he had told Fouqué:

—As for emotion, I can't quite answer; this dungeon is so ugly and damp it gives me feverish moments in which I don't recognize myself; but fear is another matter, I shall never be seen to grow pale.

He had made arrangements in advance that on the last day Fouqué should take away Mathilde and Mme. de Rênal.

—Put them in the same coach, he told him. Keep the post horses at a steady gallop. Either they will fall in one another's arms or they will fall into mortal hatred. In either case, the poor women will be somewhat distracted from their terrible grief.

Julien had forced from Mme. de Rênal an oath that she would live to look after Mathilde's son.

—Who knows? Perhaps we retain some consciousness after death, he said one day to Fouqué. I should like to rest, since rest is the word, in that little cave atop the big mountain that overlooks Verrières. I've told how several times when I spent the night in that cave and looked out over the richest provinces of France, my heart was afire with ambition: that was my passion in those days. . . . Well, that cave is precious to me, and nobody can deny that it's located in a spot that a philosopher's heart might envy. . . . You know these good congregationists in Besançon can coin money out of anything; go about it the right way, and they'll sell you my mortal remains. . . .

Julien's superb sense of humor, at the end, enchants us, but what precisely is Stendhal's final attitude towards his hero? I take this sentence as not being ironic: "Never had that head been so poetic as at the moment when it was about to fall." Julien is madly in love with Mme de Rênal; the sincerity of this madness cannot be doubted, but then the suicidal intensity or sustained drive beyond the pleasure principle of Julien's last days cannot be doubted either. Several critics have remarked upon the supposed similarity between Julien and Don Quixote, but I cannot see it. The Don lives in the order of play until he is battered out of it; then he dies. What others call madness is simply the Don's greatness. But Julien falls into pathology; it is an attractive craziness, because it makes him more likeable than before, yet it remains a kind of madness. Stendhal is poor at endings; the conclusion of *The Charterhouse of Parma* is also weak and abrupt. But I feel a certain hesitancy in myself at these judgments. Perhaps I simply like both novels so much that I resent Stendhal's own apparent loss of interest when he nears an end. The best defense of Julien's demise was made by Stendhal's subtle disciple, the Prince of Lampedusa, author of *The Leopard:* "The author hastens to kill the character in order to be free of him. It is a dramatic and evocative conclusion unlike any other." One wants to protest to the Prince that it isn't dramatic enough, but he forestalls the complaint: "The impulsive, energetic handsome Julien spends his last words to tell his friend how he must go about buying back his body." Evidently, this is dramatic in the mode of *The Leopard,* where death takes place in the soul, and the body alone remains living. A Stendhalian pathos, the Prince implies, belongs only to the happy few; it is a pathos more of sensibility than of emotion.

Mathilde and Julien, on the occasion of their first night together, are comic triumphs of sensibility over emotion. "Their transports," Stendhal observes, "were a bit *conscious,*" which is a delicious understatement:

> Mlle. de La Mole supposed she was fulfilling a duty to herself and to her lover. The poor boy, she thought to herself, he's shown perfect bravery, he ought to be happy or else the fault lies in my want of character. But she would have been glad to ransom herself, at the cost of eternal misery, from the cruel necessity imposed upon her.
>
> In spite of the frightful violence with which she repressed her feelings, she was in perfect command of her speech.
>
> No regret, no reproach came from her lips to spoil this night, which seemed strange to Julien, rather than happy. What a difference, good God! from his last stay of twenty-four hours at Verrières! These fancy Paris fashions have found a way to spoil everything, even love, he said to himself, in an excess of injustice.
>
> He was indulging in these reflections as he stood in one of the great mahogany wardrobes into which he had slipped at the first sounds coming from the next room, which was that of Mme. de La Mole. Mathilde went off with her mother to mass; the maids quickly left the room, and Julien easily escaped before they came back to finish their tasks.
>
> He took a horse and sought out the loneliest parts of the forest of Meudon near Paris. He was far more surprised than happy. The happiness that came from time to time like a gleam of light in his soul was like that of a young second lieutenant who after some astounding action has just been promoted full colonel by the commanding general; he felt himself raised to an immense height. Everything that had been far above him yesterday was now at his level or even beneath him. Gradually Julien's happiness increased as it became more remote.

If there was nothing tender in his soul, the reason, however strange it may seem, was that Mathilde in all her dealings with him had been doing nothing but her duty. There was nothing unexpected for her in all the events of the night, except the misery and shame she had discovered instead of those divine raptures that novels talk about.

Was I mistaken, don't I love him at all? she asked herself.

This hilarity of mutual coldness is the prelude to the novel's most delightful pages, as Stendhal surpasses himself in depicting the agon that springs up between these two titanic vanities. What Hobbes was to the principles of civil society, Stendhal was to the principles of eros. Neither man should be called a cynic. Each is more than a psychologist, because both saw the truth of the state of nature. Hobbes is to Stendhal what Schopenhauer was to the Tolstoy of *Anna Karenina,* the philosopher who confirms the insights so central to the novelist that they scarcely require confirmation. I would prefer to put it more starkly; if you repeatedly read *The Red and the Black,* then *Leviathan* becomes a fascinating redundancy, just as a deep knowledge of *Anna Karenina* renders *The World as Will and Representation* almost superfluous. Stendhal, and Tolstoy, are in their antithetical ways the true philosophers of love between the sexes, the dark metaphysicians of the unconscious verities of desire.

The Red and the Black: Deceit and Desire

René Girard

According to literary historians Stendhal inherited most of his ideas from the *philosophes* or the *idéologues*.

If this were true, this novelist whom we consider so great would not have a thought of his own; for his whole life he would remain faithful to the thought of others. It is a hard legend to kill. It is popular both with those who would deny intelligence in the novel and with those who are trying to find a complete Stendhalian system and think they have found it in his early writing, that is, in the only more or less didactic texts ever written by Stendhal.

Their thoughts dwell longingly on a huge key which would open all the gates of his work. A whole trousseau can be gathered effortlessly from the childish *Letters to Pauline*, from the *Journal*, and from his *New Philosophy*. There is a loud rattle in the lock but the gates remain closed. No page of *The Red and the Black* will ever be explained by means of Cabanis or Destutt de Tracy. Except for occasional borrowings from the system of temperaments there is no trace of the theories of his youth in the novels of his maturity. Stendhal is one of the few thinkers of his time who won his independence from the giants of the preceding epoch. For this reason he can render homage as an equal to the gods of his youth. Most of his romantic contemporaries are incapable of doing as much; they look on the rationalist Pantheon with great condescension, but should it enter their head to reason we find ourselves back in the century of the Enlightenment. Their opinions

From *Deceit, Desire and the Novel*, translated by Yvonne Freccero. © 1965 by the Johns Hopkins University Press, Baltimore/London.

are different and even antithetical but the intellectual frameworks have not changed.

Stendhal does not give up thinking the day he stops copying the thought of others; he begins to think for himself. If the writer had never changed his opinion on the great political and social problems, why did he declare, at the beginning of the *Life of Henry Brulard,* that he had at last decided on his point of view regarding the nobility? Nothing in the Stendhalian vision is more important than the nobility, yet this definitive point of view is never systematically set down. The real Stendhal had an aversion to didactisicm. His original thought *is* the novel and only the novel, for the moment Stendhal escapes from his characters the ghost of the Other begins to haunt him again. Therefore everything has to be gathered from his novels. The nonnovelistic texts sometimes contribute details but they should be handled with care.

Far from blindly trusting the past, Stendhal, even as early as *De L'amour,* considers the problem of the *error* in Montesquieu and other great minds of the eighteenth century. The alleged disciple wonders why such keen observers as the *philosophes* should have been so completely wrong in their visions of the future. At the end of *Memoirs of a Tourist* the theme of philosophical error is resumed and studied further. Stendhal finds nothing in Montesquieu to justify the condemnation of Louis-Philippe. The bourgeois king gave the French greater liberty and prosperity than ever before. The progress is real but it does not accord the people who benefit from it the increase of happiness foreseen by the theoreticians.

Stendhal's own duty is indicated to him by the mistakes of the *philosophes.* He must amend the conclusions of abstract intelligence by contact with experience. The intact Bastilles limited the vision of prerevolutionary thinkers. The Bastilles have fallen and the world is changing at a dizzying pace. Stendhal finds he is straddling several universes. He is observing the constitutional monarchy but he has not forgotten the *ancien régime*; he has visited England; and he keeps up with the constant stream of books dealing with the United States.

All the nations Stendhal is concerned with have embarked on the same adventure but they are moving at different speeds. The novelist is living in a veritable laboratory of historical and sociological observation. His novels are, in a sense, merely this same laboratory carried to the second degree. In them Stendhal brings together various elements which would remain isolated from each other even in the modern world. He confronts the provinces and Paris, aristocrats and bourgeois, France and Italy, and even the present and the past. Various experiments are carried out and they all have the same aim—they are all meant to answer the same fundamental question: "Why are men not happy in the modern world?"

This question is not original. Everybody, or almost everybody, was asking it in Stendhal's day. But few ask it sincerely, without having already decided a priori that one more or one less revolution is required. In his nonnovelistic writings Stendhal often seems to request both at the same time. But these secondary texts should not be allowed to worry us too much. Stendhal's real answer is blended into his novels, scattered through them; it is diffuse, full of hesitations and modifications. Stendhal is as prudent in the novels as he can be assertive, when he is expressing his own "personal" opinion in the face of the opinion of others.

Why are men not happy in the modern world? Stendhal's answer cannot be expressed in the language of political parties or of the various "social sciences." It is nonsense to both bourgeois common sense and romantic "idealism." We are not happy, says Stendhal, because we are *vaniteux.*

Morality and psychology are not the only sources of this answer. Stendhalian vanity has a historical component which is essential and which we must now clarify. In order to do this, we must first set forth Stendhal's idea of nobility, which, he tells us in the *Life of Henry Brulard,* took a solid form rather late in his development.

In Stendhal's eyes, nobility belongs to the man whose desires come from within himself and who exerts every ounce of his energy to satisfy them. Nobility, in the spiritual sense of the term, is therefore exactly synonomous with passion. The noble being rises above others by the strength of his desire. There must originally be nobility in the spiritual sense for there to be nobility in the social sense. At a certain point in history both senses of the word "noble" coincided, at least theoretically. This coincidence is illustrated in *The Italian Chronicles.* In fourteenth- and fifteenth-century Italy the greatest passions were born and developed in the elite of society.

This relative accord between the social organization and natural hierarchy of men cannot last. The nobleman's becoming aware of it is, in a sense, sufficient to precipitate its dissolution. A comparison is necessary to discover that one is superior to others: comparison means bringing closer together, putting on the same level, and, to a certain extent, treating the things compared in the same way. The equality of man cannot be denied unless it is first posited, however briefly. The oscillation between pride and shame which defines metaphysical desire can already be found in this first comparison. The nobleman who makes the comparison becomes a little more noble in the social sense but a little less noble in the spiritual sense. He begins the reflection that will gradually cut him off from his own nobility and transform it into a mere possession mediated by the *look* of the commoner. The nobleman as an individual is thus the passionate being par excellence, but nobility as a class is devoted to vanity. The more nobility is transformed into a caste and becomes hereditary, the more it closes its ranks to the passionate being who might rise from the lower classes and the more serious the ontological sickness becomes. Henceforth the nobility will be leading constantly toward vanity the other classes dedicated to its imitation and will precede them along the fatal road of metaphysical desire.

Thus the nobility is the first class to become decadent, and the history of this decadence is identical with the inevitable evolution of metaphysical desire. The nobility is already eaten up with vanity when it rushes to Versailles, drawn by the lure of vain rewards. Louis XIV is not the demigod worshipped by the royalists, nor is he the oriental tyrant loathed by the Jacobins. He is a clever politician who distrusts the aristocracy and uses its vanity as a means of government, thereby hastening the decomposition of the noble soul. The aristocracy lets itself be drawn into sterile rivalries by the monarchy which reserves the right of arbitration. The Duc de Saint-Simon, perceptive but fascinated by the king, observes with quenchless rage this emasculation of the nobility. Saint-Simon, the historian of "impotent hatred," is one of Stendhal's and Proust's great teachers.

The absolute monarchy is one stage on the road to revolution and to the most modern forms of vanity. But it is only a stage. The vanity of the court presents a strong contrast with true nobility but it makes an equally strong contrast with the vanity of the bourgeois. At Versailles the slightest desires must be approved and permitted by a whim of the King. Existence at the court is a perpetual imitation of Louis XIV. The Sun King is the mediator for all who surround him, and this mediator remains separated from his faithful followers by an immense spiritual distance. The King cannot become the rival of his own subjects. M. de Montespan would suffer much more were his wife being unfaithful to him with an ordinary mortal. The theory of "divine right" provides a perfect definition of the particular type of *external mediation* which flourishes at Versailles and in the whole of France during the last two centuries of the monarchy.

What was the state of mind of a courtier of the ancien régime, or rather what was Stendhal's impression of it? Several secondary characters in his novels and the brief but suggestive remarks scattered through some twenty works provide us with a fairly precise answer to that question. The pain caused by vanity exists in the eighteenth century but it is not unbearable. It is still possible to enjoy oneself in the protective shade of the monarchy somewhat like children at the feet of their parents. Indeed a delicate pleasure is found in mocking the futile and rigorous rules of a perpetually idle existence. The great lord has a perfect ease and grace by knowing that he is nearer the sun than other human beings and thus a little less human than they, that he is illuminated by the divine rays. He always knows exactly what to say and what not to say, what to do and what not to do. He is not afraid of being ridiculed and he gladly laughs in ridicule of others. Anything which is the slightest bit different from the latest fashion at court is ridiculous in his eyes; thus everything outside Versailles and Paris is ridiculous. It is impossible to imagine a more favorable setting for the growth of a comic theater than this universe of courtiers. Not a single allusion is lost on this public which is not many but *one*. Diderot would have been astonished to discover that laughter in the theater disappears with the "tyrant!"

The revolution destroys only one thing—but that one thing is the most important of all though it seems trivial to barren minds—the divine right of kings. After the Restoration Louis, Charles, and Philippe ascend the throne; they cling to it and descend from it more or less precipitously; only fools pay any attention to these monotonous gymnastics. The monarchy no longer exists. Stendhal insists on this fact at some length in the last part of *Lucien Leuwen*. The ceremonies at Versailles cannot turn the head of a positive-minded banker. The real power is elsewhere. And this false king, Louis-Philippe, plays the stock exchange, making himself—the ultimate downfall!—the *rival* of his own subjects!

This last touch gives us the key to the situation. The courtier's external mediation is replaced by a system of internal mediation in which the pseudo-king himself takes part. The revolutionaries thought they would be destroying vanity when they destroyed the privileges of the noble. But vanity is like a virulent cancer that spreads in a more serious form throughout the body just when one thinks it has been removed. Who is there left to imitate after the "tyrant"? Henceforth men shall copy each other; idolatry of one person is replaced by hatred of a hundred thousand rivals. In Balzac's opinions, too, there is no other god but envy for the modern crowd whose greed is no longer stemmed and held within acceptable limits by the monarch. *Men will become gods for each other.* Young men of the nobility and of the middle class come to Paris to seek their fortune as courtiers once came to Versailles. They crowd into the garrets of the Latin Quarter as once they used to pile into the attics of Versailles. Democracy is one vast middle-class court where the courtiers are everywhere and the king is nowhere. Balzac, whose observations in all these matters frequently corroborate Stendhal's, has also described this phenomenon: "In the monarchy you have

either courtiers or servants, whereas under a Charter you are served, flat-
tered and fawned on by free men." When speaking of the United States,
Tocqueville too mentions the "esprit de cour" which reigns in the democ-
racies. The sociologist's reflection throws a vivid light on the transition
from external to internal mediation:

> When all the privileges of birth and fortune have been destroyed
> so that all professions are open to everyone and it is possible to
> climb to the top by oneself, an immense and easy career seems
> available to men's ambitions, and they gladly imagine a great
> destiny for themselves. But they are mistaken, as daily experi-
> ence proves to them. The very equality which enables each cit-
> izen to sustain great hopes makes all citizens equally weak. It
> limits their strength on all sides at the same time as it allows
> their desires to spread. . . .
>
> They have destroyed the annoying privileges of some of their
> fellow-men; they encounter the competition of everyone. The
> boundary has changed its shape rather than its position. . . .
>
> The constant opposition on the one hand of instincts which
> give birth to equality and on the other of the means provided
> to satisfy them, torments and tires souls. . . . However demo-
> cratic the social state and political constitution of a nation may
> be, yet inevitably . . . each of its citizens will behold around him
> several aspects which dominate him, and it can be anticipated
> that he will obstinately fix his eyes in this one direction.

We find in Stendhal this "uneasiness" which Tocqueville attributes to
democratic regimes. The vanity of the ancien régime was gay, unconcerned,
and frivolous; the vanity of the nineteenth century is sad and suspicious; it
has a terrible fear of ridicule. "Envy, jealousy, and impotent hatred" are
the accompaniment of internal mediation. Stendhal declares that everything
has changed in a country when even fools—always the most stable element—have changed. The fool of 1780 wanted to be witty; to make people
laugh was his only ambition. The fool of 1825 wants to be serious and
formal. He is set on appearing profound and easily succeeds, the novelist
adds, because he is truly unhappy. Stendhal never tires of describing the
effects of la vanité triste on the customs and psychology of the French. The
aristocrats are most hard hit.

> When one stops considering the serious results of the revolution,
> one of the first sights that strikes one's imagination is the present

state of French society. I spent my youth among great lords who were very pleasant; today they are old, disagreeable reactionaries. At first I thought their peevish humor was an unfortunate effect of age, so I made the acquaintance of their children who will inherit great wealth and noble titles, in fact most of the privileges that men drawn together in society can confer on some among them; I found them sunk even deeper in despondency than their parents.

The transition from external to internal mediation constitutes the supreme phase in the decline of the nobility. Revolution and emigration completed what reflection had begun; the nobleman, physically separated from his privileges, is henceforth forced to see them for what they really are—*arbitrary.* Stendhal clearly understood that the revolution could not destroy the nobility by taking away its privileges. But the nobility could destroy itself by desiring that of which it had been deprived by the bourgeoisie, and by devoting itself to the ignoble sentiments of internal mediation. To realize that the privilege is arbitrary and to still desire it is obviously the height of vanity. The noble thinks he is defending his nobility by fighting for its privileges against the other classes of a nation but he only succeeds in ruining it. He desires to recuperate his wealth as a bourgeois might and the envy of the bourgeoisie stimulates his desire and endows the pettiest of honorary trifles with immense value. Mediated by each other, henceforth the two classes will desire the same things in the same way. The Restoration duke who regains his titles and fortune, thanks to the millions granted to the *émigrés,* is little more than a bourgeois "who won in the lottery." The nobleman constantly grows nearer the bourgeois, even in the hatred he feels for him. They are all ignoble, Stendahl writes somewhat strongly in his letter to Balzac, *because they prize nobility.*

Only their elegant manners and politeness, the results of long training, give the nobles a little distinction over the bourgeoisie, and even this will soon disappear. Double mediation is a melting-pot in which differences among classes and individuals gradually dissolve. It functions all the more efficiently because it does not even appear to affect diversity. In fact, the latter is even given a fresh though deceptive brilliance: the opposition of the Same to the Same, which flourishes everywhere, will hide itself for a long time to come behind traditional diversity, sheltering new conflicts behind the shadow of old ones and nourishing belief in the integral survival of the past.

Under the Restoration the nobility seems more alive than ever. Never have its privileges been more desired, nor its ancient families so eager to emphasize the barriers between themselves and the common people. Superficial observers are not aware that internal mediation is at work; they can only conceive uniformity as that of marbles in a bag or sheep in a meadow. They do not recognize the modern tendency to identity in passionate divisions, their own divisions. But the clash of cymbals is loudest when they fit each other exactly.

Because it is no longer distinct the aristocracy tries to distinguish itself, and it succeeds marvelously—but that does not make it any more noble. It is a fact, for instance, that under the constitutional monarchy the aristocracy is the stuffiest and most virtuous class in the nation. The frivolous and seductive nobleman of the Louis XV era has been replaced by the scowling and morose gentleman of the Restoration. This depressing character lives on his property, he works hard, goes to bed early, and worst of all, even manages to economize. What is the significance of such austere morals? Is it really a return to the "ancestral virtues"? This is what we are told constantly in the *bien-pensant* journals but there is no need to believe it. This gloomy, sour-tempered, and totally negative kind of wisdom is typically bourgeois. The aristocracy is trying to prove to the Others that it has "earned" its privileges; that is why it borrows its code of ethics from the class which is competing for those same privileges. Mediated by its bourgeois audience, the nobility copies the bourgeoisie without even realizing it. In *Memoirs of a Tourist* Stendhal remarks sardonically that the revolution has bequeathed to the French aristocracy the customs of democratic, protestant Geneva.

Thus their very hatred of the bourgeoisie makes them middle-class. And, since mediation is reciprocal, we must expect to find a bourgeois-gentleman to match the gentleman-bourgeois, we must anticipate a bourgeois comedy which is symmetrical and inverse to the aristocratic comedy. The courtiers may copy Rousseau's *vicaire savoyard* in order to capture the good opinion of the bourgeois, but the bourgeois will also play at being great lords to impress the aristocrats. The type of the bourgeois imitator reaches the height of comic perfection in the character of Baron Nerwinde in *Lamiel*. Nerwinde, the son of a general of the Empire, slavishly and laboriously copies a synthetic model, made up in equal parts of a *roué* of the ancien régime and a dandy from across the Channel. Nerwinde leads a tedious and boring existence, but its very disorder he has organized methodically. He goes bankrupt conscientiously while keeping very exact accounts. He does it all to make people forget—and to make himself forget—that he is the grandson of a hatter from Périgueux.

Double mediation flourishes everywhere; there is a "set to partners" in every figure of Stendhal's social ballet. Everything is reversed from its previous state. Stendhal's wit amuses us but it seems a little too geometric to be true. It is important to note that Tocqueville, who is a completely humorless observer, makes assertions parallel to Stendhal's. In *The Ancient Regime and the Revolution,* for instance, we find the paradox of an aristocracy that by its opposition to the middle class begins to resemble it, and that adopts all the virtues of which the middle class is trying to rid itself. He writes: "The most antidemocratic classes of the nation reveal most clearly to us the kind of morality it is reasonable to expect from a democracy."

When the aristocracy seems most alive is precisely when it is most dead. In an early edition of *Lamiel* Nerwinde is called D'Aubigné; this imitative dandy belonged to the aristocracy, not to the parvenu middle class: he was a descendant of Mme de Maintenon. Otherwise his conduct was exactly the same as in the last version of the novel. No doubt Stendhal chose the parvenu bourgeois—the commoner—to play the comedy of the nobility because he felt that the comic effect would be more apparent and reliable, but this does not mean he was mistaken in the first version; it illustrates an essential aspect of the Stendhalian truth. In that case it was a nobleman by blood who played the comedy of nobility. With or without a coat-of-arms, one can "desire" nobility, under Louis-Philippe, only in the manner of Molière's *bourgeois gentilhomme.* One can only mime it, as passionately as M. Jourdain but less naïvely. It is this kind of mimicry which Stendhal is trying to reveal to us. The complexity of the task and the fragmentation of the public—which are, ultimately, one and the same phenomenon—make the theater unsuited to carrying out this literary function. Comic theater died with the monarchy and "gay vanity." A more flexible genre is needed to describe the infinite metamorphoses of *vanité triste* and reveal how void are its oppositions. This genre is the novel. Stendhal finally understood this; after long years of effort and failure, which transformed his soul, he gave up the theater. But he never renounced his ambition of becoming a great comic writer. All novelistic works have a tendency to the comic and Stendhal's are no exception Flaubert excels himself in *Bouvard et Pécuchet;* Proust reaches his peak in the comic figure of the Baron Charlus; Stendhal sums up and completes his work in the great comic scenes of *Lamiel.*

The paradox of an aristocracy that becomes democratic through its very hatred of democracy is nowhere more striking than in political life. The tendency of the nobility to become bourgeois is clearly seen in its sympathy for the *ultra* party, a party devoted entirely to the defense of privilege; this party's conflict with Louis XVIII showed clearly that the monarch was no longer the polar star of the nobility but a political instrument in the hands of the noble party. This noble party is oriented not toward the king but toward the rival bourgeoisie. The *ultra* ideology is merely the pure and simple reversal of revolutionary ideology. The theme throughout is *reaction* and reveals the negative slavery of internal mediation. Party rule is the natural political expression of this mediation; party platforms do not bring about political opposition—opposition brings about party platforms.

To understand how ignoble ultracism is, it must be compared with a form of thought which was anterior to the revolution and which, in its time, convinced a whole section of the nobility: the philosophy of the Enlightenment. Stendhal believes that this philosophy is the only one possible for nobility that intends to remain noble in the exercise of its thought. When a genuine aristocrat—and there were still a few during the last century of the monarchy—enters the territory of thought, he does not abandon his native virtues. He remains spontaneous even in his reflection. Unlike the ultras he does not expect the ideas he adopts to serve the interests of his class, any more than he would ask a challenger, in a truly heroic era, to present proof of nobility; the challenge alone would prove the nobility of the challenger, in the eyes of someone with self-respect. In the realm of thought rational evidence takes the place of the challenge. The nobleman accepts the challenge and judges everything in universal terms. He goes straight to the most general truths and applies them to all mankind. He does not acknowledge any exceptions, especially those from which he would profit. In Montesquieu, and in the best of the enlightened nobles of the eighteenth century, there is no distinction between the aristocratic and the liberal mind. Eighteenth-century rationalism is noble even in its illusions; it puts its trust in "human nature." It does not allow for the irrational in human relations, nor does it recognize metaphysical imitation, which frustrates the calculations of sound reflection. Montesquieu would have been less likeable had he foreseen the *vanité triste* of the nineteenth century.

Moreover, we soon realize that rationalism means the death of privilege. Truly noble reflection resigns itself to that death, just as the truly noble warrior is prepared to die on the battlefield. The nobility cannot reflect on itself and remain noble without destroying itself as a caste; and since the revolution forced the nobility to think about itself, its own extinction is the only choice left to it. The nobility can die nobly by the one and only political gesture worthy of it, the destruction of its own privileged existence—the night August 4, 1789. (During the night the deputies of the aristocracy at the revolutionary *Assemblée constituante* voted the abolition of most feudal privileges.) It dies meanly, in a bourgeois fashion, on the benches of some House of Lords, confronted by Valenods whom it ends up resembling through fighting with them over the spoils. This was the solution of the ultras.

First came the nobility; then followed the noble class; finally only a noble party is left. After the period when the two coincided, spiritual and social nobility now tend to exclude each other; henceforth the incompatibility of privilege with greatness of soul is so radical that it is patent even in the attempts to conceal it. Take for example the justification of privilege given by Dr. du Périer, the intellectual jack-of-all-trades of the Nancy nobility:

> A man is born a duke, a millionaire and a peer of France, it is not for him to consider whether his position conforms with virtue, or with the general good or with other fine ideas. His position is good; so he should do everything to maintain and improve it, or be despised generally as a coward and a fool.

Du Périer would like to convince us that the nineteenth-century nobleman is still living in a happy era, not yet affected by the "look" of the Other, still enjoying his privileges spontaneously. Yet the lie is so flagrant that Du Périer does not phrase it directly; he uses a negative periphrasis that suggests without affirming: "It is not for him to consider," etc. Despite this oratorical precaution, the "look" of the Other is too obsessive and Du Périer is forced to acknowledge it in the following sentence. But then he imagines a cynical point of honor to which this "look" forces the aristocrat to submit. If the privileged person does not hang on to his privilege, "he will be despised as a coward or a fool." Du Périer is once again lying. Aristocrats are neither innocent nor cynical: they are merely *vaniteux*; they want privilege merely as parvenus. This is the horrible truth which must be hidden at all cost. They are ignoble *because they prize nobility*.

Since the Revolution no one can be privileged without knowing it. Stendhal's kind of hero is impossible in France. Stendhal likes to believe that he is still just possible in Italy. In that happy country, scarcely touched by the Revolution, reflection and concern with the Other have not yet completely poisoned enjoyment of the world and of oneself. A truly heroic soul is still compatible with the privileged circumstances which allow him free play. Fabrice del Dongo can be spontaneous and generous in the midst of an injustice from which he benefits.

First we see Fabrice flying to the aid of an emperor who embodies the spirit of the Revolution; a little later we find our hero, haughty, devout, and aristocratic, in the Italy of his childhood. Fabrice does not think for a minute he is "demeaning" himself when he challenges a simple soldier of the glorious imperial army to a duel. Yet he speaks harshly to the servant who risks his life for him. Still later, despite his devotion, he does not hesitate to join in the simoniac intrigues which will make him an archbishop of Parma. Fabrice is not a hypocrite, nor does he lack intelligence; he is merely lacking the historical foundations for the ability to reflect. The comparisons which a privileged young Frenchman would be forced to make never even enter his mind.

The French will never recover the innocence of a Fabrice for *it is not possible to move backward in the order of the passions*. Historic and psychic evolution are irreversible. Stendhal finds the Restoration revolting but not because he sees in it naïvely a "return to the *ancien régime*." Such a return is unthinkable; moreover, Louis XVIII's Charter marks the first concrete step toward democracy "since 1792." The current interpretation of *The Red and the Black* therefore is inadmissible. The Jacobin novel described in the handbooks of literature does not exist. If Stendhal were writing for all those bourgeois who are temporarily cut off from lucrative careers by the temporary triumph of an absolutist and feudal party, his would be a very clumsy work. Traditional interpretations go counter to the most basic tenets of the author and disregard the *facts* of the novel, among which is the brilliant career of Julien. One might object that this career is broken by the reactionary and clerical *Congrégation* (a secret Catholic organization with great political influence). True, yet this same *Congrégation* a little later makes every effort to save the protégé of the Marquis de la Mole. Julien is not so much the victim of the ultras as of the wealthy and jealous bourgeois who will triumph in July, 1830. Moreover, we should not look for any partisan lesson in Stendhal's masterpieces—to understand this novelist who is always talking politics we must free ourselves of political ways of thinking.

Julien has a brilliant career which he owes to M. de la Mole. In his article on *The Red and the Black* Stendhal describes the latter in these words: "His character as nobleman was not formed by the revolution of 1794." In other words, M. de la Mole retains some genuine nobility; he has not become middle-class through hatred of the middle class. His freedom of thought has not made him a democrat but it prevents him from being a reactionary in the worst sense of the word. M. de la Mole does not depend exclusively on excommunications, negations, and refusals; ultracism and the nobleman's reaction have not smothered all other sentiments in him. His wife and his friends judge men only by their birth, their fortune, and their political orthodoxy, and so would a Valenod in their place; but M. de la Mole is still capable of approving the rise of a talented commoner. He proves it with Julien Sorel. Only once does Stendhal find his character vulgar—when he loses his temper at the thought that his daughter, by marrying Julien, will never be a duchess.

Julien owes his success to that element under the new regime which has most truly survived from the ancien régime. This is a strange way for Stendhal to campaign against a return to the past; even if the novelist had shown the failure of the numerous young people who did not have the good fortune to meet their Marquis de la Mole, his novel would still not have proved anything against the ancien régime. In fact is it the Revolution which has increased the obstacles, since most people with status owe "their character of noblemen"—i.e., their implacable ultracism—to the Revolution.

Must then the obstacle in the way of these young people be called democratic? Is not this an empty subtlety, and even an untenable paradox? Surely it is only fair that the bourgeoisie should take over the controls since it is "the most energetic and active class in the nation." Is it not true that a little more "democracy" would smooth the way for the ambitious?

It is true; in any case, the stupidity of the ultras makes their downfall inevitable. But Stendhal looks further. The political elimination of the noble party cannot reestablish harmony and satisfy the desires that have been awakened. The political conflict which rages under the constitutional monarchy is considered the sequel of a great historic drama, the last thunderclaps of a storm that is moving away. The revolutionaries suppose they must clear the ground and make a fresh start; Stendhal is telling them that they have already started. Ancient historic appearances hide a new structure of human relations. The party struggle is rooted not in past inequality, but in the present equality, no matter how imperfect it may be.

The historical justification of the internal struggles is scarcely more than a pretext now. Put aside the pretext and the true cause will appear. Ultracism will disappear like liberalism, but internal mediation remains; and internal mediation will never be lacking in excuses for maintaining the division into rival camps. Following religious society, civic society has become schismatic. To look forward optimistically to the democratic future under the pretext that the ultras, or their successors, are destined to disappear from the political scene is once again to put the object before the mediator and desire before envy. This error can be compared to that of the chronic sufferer from jealousy who always thinks his illness will be cured when the current rival is eliminated.

The last century of French history has proved Stendhal right. The party struggle is the only stable element in contemporary instability. Principles no longer cause rivalry; it is a metaphysical rivalry, which slips into contrary principles like mollusks that nature has not provided with shells and that install themselves in the first ones to come along, no matter what kind.

Proof of this can be furnished by the pair Rênal-Valenod. M. de Rênal abandons ultracism before the 1827 elections. He has himself entered as a candidate on the liberal ticket. Jean Prévost discovers in this sudden conversion proof that even Stendhal's secondary characters are capable of "surprising" the reader. Prévost, usually so perspicacious, in this point has fallen victim to the pernicious myths of the "true to life" and "spontaneity" which plague literary criticism.

Julien smiles when he learns of the political about-face of his former patron—he knows very well that nothing has changed. Once more it is a question of playing a role opposite Valenod. The latter has gotten in the good graces of the *Congrégation;* he will therefore be the ultras' candidate. For M. de Rênal there is nothing left to do but turn toward those liberals who seemed so formidable to him a few years before. We meet the mayor of Verrières again in the last pages of the novel. He introduces himself pompously as a "liberal of the defection," but from his second sentence on he merely echoes Valenod. Submission to the Other is no less absolute when it assumes negative forms—a puppet is no less a puppet when the strings are crossed. With regard to the virtues of opposition Stendhal does not share in the optimism of a Hegel or of our contemporary "rebels."

The figure cut by the two businessmen of Verrières was not perfect so long as they both belonged to the same political party. Double mediation demanded M. de Rênal's conversion to liberalism. There was a need for symmetry which had not yet been fulfilled. And that final *entrechat* was needed to bring to a proper end the ballet of Rênal-Valenod, which was being performed in a corner of the stage all through *The Red and the Black.*

Julien savors the "conversion" of M. de Rênal as a music lover who sees a melodic theme reappear under a new orchestral disguise. Most men are taken in by the disguises. Stendhal places a smile on Julien's lips so that his readers should not be deceived. He does not want us to be fooled: he wants to turn our attention away from the objects and fix it on the mediator; he wishes to reveal to us the genesis of desire, to teach us to distinguish true freedom from the negative slavery which caricatures it. If we take M. de Rênal's liberalism seriously we are destroying the very essence of *The Red and the Black* and reducing a work of genius to the proportions of a Victor Cousin or a Saint-Marc Girardin.

M. de Rênal's conversion is the first act of a political tragicomedy which excites the enthusiasm of naive spectators throughout the nineteenth century. First the actors exchange threats, then they exchange roles. They leave the stage and return in a new costume. Behind this perpetually similar but different spectacle the same opposition continues to exist, becoming ever more empty and yet more ferocious. And internal mediation continues its underground work.

The political thinkers of our time are always seeking in Stendhal an echo of their own thoughts. They recreate a revolutionary Stendhal or a reactionary Stendhal according to their own passions. But the shroud is never large enough to cover the corpse. Aragon's Stendhal is no more satisfactory than that of Maurice Barrès or Charles Maurras. One line of the writer's own suffices to bring the weak ideological scaffoldings tumbling down into the void: "As regards extreme parties," we read in the preface to *Lucien Leuwen*, "it is always those we have seen most recently which seem the most ridiculous."

The youthful Stendhal most certainly leaned toward the republicans. The mature Stendhal is not lacking in sympathy for the incorruptible Catoes who, deaf to Louis-Philippe's objurgations, refuse to grow rich and are preparing in the shadows a new revolution. But we must not confuse with political affiliation this very particular feeling of sympathy. The problem is discussed at length in *Lucien Leuwen* and the position of the later Stendhal—the Stendhal who carries most weight—is in no way ambiguous.

We must seek among the austere republicans whatever is left of nobility in the political arena. Only these republicans still hope for the destruction of all forms of vanity. They retain the eighteenth-century illusion concerning the excellence of human nature. They have understood neither the revolution nor *vanité triste*. They do not realize that the most beautiful fruits of ideological thought will always be spoiled by the worm of irrationality. These men of integrity do not have the *philosophes'* excuse of living *before* the Revolution; thus they are much less intelligent than Montesquieu, and they are much less amusing. If their hands were free, they would create a regime identical with that which flourishes under republican, protestant puritanism in the state of New York. Individual rights would be respected; prosperity would be assured, but the last refinements of aristocratic existence would disappear; vanity would take an even baser form than under the constitutional monarchy. Stendhal concludes that it is less distressing to flatter a Talleyrand or even a minister of Louis-Philippe's than to pay court "to one's shoemaker."

Stendhal is an atheist in politics, a fact hard to believe either in his day or in ours. Despite the levity of its manifestations this atheism is not a frivolous skepticism but a profound conviction. Stendhal does not evade problems; his point of view is the outcome of a whole life of meditation. But it is a point of view which will never be understood by party-minded people nor by many other people who unconsciously are influenced by the party spirit. An ambiguous homage is paid to the novelist's thought, which secretly denies its coherence. It is considered "impulsive" and "disconcerting." It is full of "whims" and "paradoxes." The unfortunate writer is lucky if "a double heritage, both aristocratic and popular" is not invoked which would tear him apart. Let us leave to Mérimée the image of a Stendhal dominated by the spirit of contradiction and we shall understand perhaps that Stendhal is accusing *us* and our time of self-contradiction.

As usual, if we are to have a better understanding of the novelist's thought, we should compare it with a later work which will amply justify its perspectives and will make even its more daring aspects seem banal, merely by revealing a more advanced stage of metaphysical desire. In Stendhal's case, we must ask Flaubert to provide us with a key. Although Emma Bovary's desire still belongs to the area of external mediation, Flaubert's universe as a whole, and especially the urban life of *The Sentimental Education,* are the result of an internal mediation which is even more extreme than that of Stendhal. Flaubert's mediation exaggerates the characteristics of Stendhalian mediation and draws a caricature of it that is much easier for us to figure out than the original.

The environment of *The Sentimental Education* is the same as that of *The Red and the Black.* Again the provinces and Paris are opposed to one another, but it is clear that the center of gravity has moved toward Paris, the capital of desire, which increasingly polarizes the vital forces of the nation. Relationships between people remain the same and enable us to measure the progress of internal mediation. M. de la Mole has been replaced by M. Dambreuse, a "liberal" who owes his character of rapacious big banker as much to 1830 as to 1794. Mathilde is succeeded by the venal Mme Dambreuse. Julien Sorel is followed by a whole crowd of young men who come, like him, to "conquer" the capital. They are less talented but more greedy. Chances of success are not wanting but everybody wants the most "conspicuous" position, and the front row can never be stretched far since it owes its position purely to the inevitably limited attention of the crowd. The number of those who are called increases constantly but the number of the elect does not. Flaubert's ambitious man never attains the object of his desires. He knows neither the real misery nor the real despair caused by possession and disillusionment. His horizon never grows wider. He is doomed to bitterness, malice, and petty rivalries. Flaubert's novel confirms Stendhal's dire prediction on the future of the bourgeois.

The opposition between the ambitious younger men and those who are successful grows ever more bitter although there are no more ultras. The intellectual basis of the oppositions is even more ridiculous and unstable than in Stendhal. If there is a victor in this bourgeois *cursus honorum* described in *The Sentimental Education* then it is Martinon, the most insipid of the characters and the biggest schemer, who corresponds, though he is even duller witted, to little Tambeau of *The Red and the Black.* The democratic court which has replaced that of the monarchy grows larger, more anonymous, and more unjust. Unfit for true freedom, Flaubert's characters are always attracted by what attracts their fellow men. They can desire only what the Others desire. The priority of rivalry over desire inevitably increases the amount of suffering caused by vanity.

Flaubert too is an atheist in politics. If we make allowance for the differences of time and temperament, his attitude is amazingly similar to that of Stendhal. This spiritual relationship becomes more apparent on reading Tocqueville: the sociologist, too, is immunized against partisan positions, and the best of his work almost succeeds in providing the systematic expression of an historical and political truth which often remains implicit in the great works of the two novelists.

The increasing equality—the approach of the mediator in our terms—does not give rise to harmony but to an even keener rivalry. Although this rivalry is the source of considerable material benefits, it also leads to even more considerable spiritual sufferings, for nothing material can appease it. Equality which alleviates poverty is in itself good but it cannot satisfy even those who are keenest in demanding it; it only exasperates their desire. When he emphasises the vicious circle in which the passion for equality is trapped, Tocqueville reveals an essential aspect of triangular desire. The ontological sickness, we know, always leads its victims toward the "solutions" that are most likely to aggravate it. The passion for equality is a madness unequalled except by the contrary and symmetrical passion for inequality, which is even more abstract and contributes even more directly to the unhappiness caused by freedom in those who are incapable of accepting it in a manly fashion. Rival ideologies merely reflect both the unhappiness and the incapability; thus they result from internal mediation—rival ideologies owe their power of persuasion only to the secret support the opposing factions lend each other. Fruits of the ontological scission, their duality reflects its unhuman geometry and in return they provide food for the devouring rivalry.

Stendhal, Flaubert, Tocqueville describe as "republican" or "democratic" an evolution which we today would call *totalitarian*. As the mediator comes nearer and the concrete differences between men grow smaller, abstract opposition plays an ever larger part in individual and collective existence. All the forces of being are gradually organized into twin structures whose opposition grows ever more exact. Thus every human force is braced in a struggle that is as relentless as it is senseless, since no concrete difference or positive value is involved. Totalitarianism is precisely this. The social and political aspects of this phenomenon cannot be distinguished from its personal and private aspects. Totalitarianism exists when all desires have been organized one by one into a general and permanent mobilization of being in the service of nothingness.

Balzac often treats very seriously the oppositions he sees around him; Stendhal and Flaubert, on the other hand, always point out their futility. In the work of these two authors, this double structure is embodied in "cerebral love," political struggles, petty rivalries among businessmen and the notables of the provinces. Starting from these particular areas, it is the truly schismatic tendency of romantic and modern society which in each case is demonstrated. But Stendhal and Flaubert did not foresee, and no doubt could not foresee, where this tendency would lead humanity. Double mediation has invaded the growing domain of collective existence and wormed its way into the more intimate depths of the individual soul, until finally it stretches beyond national boundaries and annexes countries, races, and continents, in the heart of a universe where technical progress is wiping away one by one the differences between men. Stendhal and Flaubert underestimated the extent to which triangular desire might expand, perhaps because they lived too early, or perhaps because they did not see clearly its metaphysical nature. Whatever the reason, they did not foresee the at once cataclysmic yet insignificant conflicts of the twentieth century. They perceived the grotesque element of the era which was about to begin but they did not suspect its tragedy.

The Red and the Black:
Social Originality

Harry Levin

As a psychological novelist, Stendhal had many models; as a social novelist, he had few. There had been a few fumbling attempts to deal realistically with provincial life, and he had manifested an interest in them. For Mortonval's *Tartuffe moderne,* with its glimpse into the petty politics of a theological seminary, he had his obvious uses. Lemontey's *Famille de Jura,* with its regional setting and its peasant's impression of Paris, was more of a Bonapartist pamphlet than a novel, and all the more stimulating on that account. More and more suspicious of novels, Stendhal had grown particularly fond of memoirs. It is no coincidence that a remarkable triad of human documents—from the courtier Saint-Simon, the philanderer Casanova, and the detective Vidocq—first saw print within a year or two before *Le Rouge et le noir.* In Italian libraries, where he spent long hours copying anecdotes and *novelle* out of Renaissance manuscripts, Stendhal discovered immense reserves of energy. Splendid sinners, like Francesco Cenci or Vittoria Accoramboni, set examples for his characters; and forgotten chroniclers plied a lively, unvarnished, economical style which he has preserved in such Italianate tales as *L'Abbesse de Castro.* His distrust of imagination made him peculiarly dependent upon documentation; this dependence, in this early writing, did not quite stop short of plagiary. He took his property, like Molière, where he found it, and where the Elizabethan dramatists found their subjects. He might have avowed, with André Gide, "I have never been able to invent anything." It was Stendhal who introduced novelists to the habit of clipping their material out of news-

From *The Gates of Horn.* © 1963 by Harry Levin. Oxford University Press, 1963.

papers, particularly out of the crime news. There he came across the case of Antoine Berthet, a student of theology employed as a tutor, who had made advances to one employer's wife and another's daughter; who, having been dismissed, had attempted murder and suicide; and who had then been tried and condemned to death by a court at Grenoble in 1827.

There, unsuspectedly close to home, were the facts, the little true facts, the "odious truths" that would shock Mérimée. The problem was whether the techniques of fiction were adequate to handle them. The most available genre was that which the Waverley novels had so successfully exploited. "The French nation is mad about Walter Scott," Stendhal had declared, counting two hundred translations and adaptations and imitations. Young writers were trying their hands at historical novels: Vigny with *Cinq-Mars* in 1826, Balzac with *Les Chouans* in 1829, Hugo with *Notre-Dame de Paris* in 1831. Mérimée, who stood closest to Stendhal, made the Saint Bartholomew massacre a theme for anticlerical satire with his 1572, *Chronique du règne de Charles IX,* which appeared in 1829. In 1830 several chapters from *Le Rouge et le noir* appeared in periodicals, subtitled *Chronique de 1830.* The year, and the completion of the book, were interrupted by the July Revolution; the subtitle, to retain its element of timeliness, became *Chronique du dix-neuvième siècle.* So timely was the book that, although it covers its hero's life from his nineteenth through his twenty-third year, an early chapter is headed "Modes of Behavior in 1830." In an anonymous puff Stendhal praised himself for daring "to recount an adventure which took place in 1830." The most original feature of *Armance* had likewise been the note struck by its subtitle, *Quelques Scènes d'un salon en 1827;* not only was 1827 the date of publication, but *scènes* was a hint which Balzac would act upon. Stendhal's journalistic timing, his emphatic contemporaneity, contrasts strikingly with the work of Scott's imitators. In an essay on Scott and *La Princesse de Clèves* he demurred:

> *Imitate nature* is a piece of advice which is devoid of meaning. To what extent must one imitate nature in order to please the reader? That is the big question. . . . If art is nothing but a beautiful lie, Sir Walter Scott has been too much of a liar.

But this dismissal is cavalierly unfair to the most influential of novelists. As an antiquarian and a tourist, Scott had broadened the picaresque novel by taking history and geography in his stride; by taking a comprehensive survey of a given region of the past, from court to cottage, he had paved the way for the sociological novel. Stendhal's contribution—to take the present for his period, to write a historical novel of his own time was, in the judgment of a recent Italian critic, "the most important literary inno-vation of the century." From the introductory epigraph—Danton's phrase, "bitter truth"—Stendhal gives an unprecedented twist to Scott's conven-tions. We start from the usual topographical presentation: the little village of Verrières, its red-tiled roofs and its Spanish ruins, the Jura mountains in the background and the river Doubs in the foreground. Then, as the river turns, the tempo changes: water-power, industry, textiles, machines, the fall of Napoleon, and the rise of the bourgeoisie as typified by the figure of the mayor, M. de Rênal. Two further chapters of small-town gossip and business prepare us for a close-up of Julien Sorel, sitting astride a beam in his father's sawmill and reading *Le Mémorial de Sainte-Hélène.*

The novel develops, under ideological auspices, into a case study of Antoine Berthet's motivation, an analysis of the interaction between tem-perament and environment. For literary purposes the hero is drawn some-what larger than life, and draped in the attributes of a vestigial romanticism. Like Byron's Manfred, he is attended by an ominous bird; like Lamartine's Jocelyn, he repairs at intervals to a mysterious grotto; but under his sem-inarist's garb, he is not an angel; he is another *homme fatal.* His fatality, rationally considered, is that of Dumas's Antony or Hugo's Ruy Blas: to be qualified for a dominant role and cast in a subordinate position. But narrative, unlike drama, can present itself through the hero's point of view; and when the hero happens to occupy a domestic position, we can expect an inside story which will upset the more conventional views. Julien is constantly citing the precedent of Saint-Preux, a tutor, and of Rousseau himself, an erstwhile lackey. Julien's knowledge of the world has been precariously gleaned from the *Confessions.* Stendhal's, by this time, is wider. His task is to present his romantic hero in a realistic situation, to inject a confession into his chronicle. Las Cases's *Mémorial de Sainte-Hélène,* being Napoleon's confession and chronicle, is Julien's inevitable favorite among many books. It does not matter that his father knocks it into the mill-race, for Julien has memorized it more assiduously than the New Testament. The old army surgeon, who bequeathed it to him, was the only person toward whom he has been able to behave sincerely; and he uses a surrep-titious portrait of Napoleon as a test of Madame de Rênal's sincerity. He cannot take a step without wondering what "the other one" would have done in his shoes; he prepares himself for his amatory conquests by rereading the bulletins of the Grand Army. What will happen, without the Emperor, to those poor devils who have just enough money for an education and not enough for a career? "Whatever happens," Julien muses, "that fatal memory will prevent us from being happy."

Stendhal recollected, in the preface to *Armance,* an operatic snatch hummed by Napoleon during the Russian campaign: "Whether to be a miller or a notary. . . . " It must have seemed, to the young men he led to glory, that the choice was infinite. In those days, some fifteen years before, one was either dead or a general at thirty-six. A glance at the Sixth Dragoons returning from Italy—Stendhal's own regiment—awakens Julien's military ambitions. But his pale and perfervid generation, which Musset interpreted six years after Stendhal in *La Confession d'un enfant du siècle,* a generation whose infant slumbers were broken by the tramp of the returning armies, whose boyish dreams were pervaded by the sands of Egypt and the snows of Russia, was to be bitterly disillusioned: "When children talked of glory, they were told, 'Enter the priesthood.' " The cassock was their "terrible symbol." Hence Julien's boast: "I know how to choose the uniform of my century." The eagles have disappeared; the only career still open to talent is the church. Julien is constrained to hide his worship of Jean-Jacques and Bonaparte; a set of Tacitus, the present of the worldly old bishop of Besançon, is his *moyen de parvenir;* Maistre's *Du Pape,* the manual of ultramontane Catholicism, is his careerist's handbook. In the lottery of fortune he plays the alternatives of red and black—the colors of revolution and reaction, the uniforms of the army and the clergy, the genuine ardor that burns in his breast and the cold careerism that governs his conduct. Never is he more himself than in the scene at the restored abbey of Bray-le-Haut. He has ridden in the king's guard of honor, and he feels his spurs beneath his subdiaconal garments. The young bishop of Agde, another clerical career man, performs the benediction that Julien has watched him rehearse before a mirror. The cannoneers, veterans of the Battle of Leipzig, fire a salute. The whole ceremony costs 3800 francs, and undoes the work of a hundred Jacobin papers.

Le Rouge et le noir is a funeral eulogy over the lost generation that was born during the Empire and came of age under the Restoration. Clericalism has thrown a pall over their hopes. "Under Napoleon, I should have been a sergeant; among these future *curés* I shall be a vicar-general," so the neophyte resolves, when he finds the seminary filled with crass peasants whose sole concern is a comfortable living. Though he is not insensitive to the attractions of religion, though he delights in decorating the cathedral, his brain is too clear to be fuddled by the incense of Chateaubriand's religiosity. He finds, to his surprise, that some priests are sincerely religious; but they are Jansenists like his austere mentor, the Abbé Pirard, suspected of heresy and persecuted by their blackrobed brethren. The kindly Chélan, who doubts if Julien's vocation is sincere, loses his parish because he has allowed a reformer to inspect the prison. No local graft is too small and no national policy is too big for the machinations of the Jesuits: from appointing a bigoted imbecile to the lottery office—and ignoring the worthier candidate, Stendhal's old friend Gros—to conspiring with the enemies of France for the return of ecclesiastical property—and making Julien, somewhat anachronistically, the bearer of the notorious secret note that urged the Duke of Wellington to prolong the foreign occupation. The plot is controlled, behind the scenes, by the political strategy of the Jesuit-dominated Congregation; the wires are pulled, from first to last, by its director, the vicar-general Frilair. *Lamiel* continues the exposure with a grotesque account of a Jesuit mission, where a sermon is heightened by fireworks. Stendhal's account of the pageantry at Bray-le-Haut echoes the coronation of Charles X, last of the Bourbons and most extreme of the ultras, at Rheims in 1825—an occasion on which Church and State had managed to travesty one another.

The reign of counterrevolutionary terror thus heralded, which did its utmost to revoke the charter of 1815, to repress the liberties that the Revolution had extended and to restore the privileges it had abolished, is the occasion of Stendhal's novel. Needless to say, the novel could hardly have been printed until that reign was over, and its harsh restrictions on the press had been lifted. Hence Stendhal's climax is appropriately staged in a newly built church during the celebration of the mass. Julien's pistol seems to be specifically aimed at the Jesuitical legislation against sacrilege; the blasphemous reverberations seem to celebrate the downfall of Bourbons and ultras. The Three Glorious Days of the July Revolution were generally likened to the Glorious Revolution that drove the Stuarts from the English throne. The opening chapter of the second volume, wherein the mailcoach brings Julien from country to city, is a debate between a Bonapartist and a Liberal, who speak for the previous and the succeeding regimes. The two volumes proceed, in ascending order, from the provincial bourgeoisie to the Parisian aristocracy, while Julien proceeds from tutor to seminarist and from secretary to officer. In each of the two households that employ him, the servant asserts his mastery through sex; first Louise de Rênal, and then Mathilde de La Mole, becomes his mistress. The ladder, which he formerly climbed to decorate an altar, becomes an accessory to his love affairs and a symbol of his ascent in the social hierarchy. His successive masters, M. de Rênal and the Marquis de La Mole, find him an apt pupil; for his part, he finds that the difference between chicanery and diplomacy is a matter of scale. In the first excitement of arrival, and the constant fear of ridicule, he expects too much; overeager to do the correct thing, he makes the mistake of challenging a coachman. Experience is disappointment: when he has fought a real duel, and when he has accomplished his first seduction, his comment is "N'est-ce que ça?"

Passion is intermingled with politics in Stendhal; his lovers are usually members of different parties or antagonistic classes; his projected comedy, *Les Deux Hommes,* pitted the republican character against the monarchic. Julien, as a lover, is the man of energy converting his force into heat, the Jacobin turned social climber. The author of *De l'amour* understood that love, in its incipient stages, is almost indistinguishable from self-love. Julien's *devoir* is primarily a sense of what he owes to himself. When he deliberately grasps Louise's hand, and she impulsively responds, he begins to realize that love has its unselfish aspects. He is not lying when he tells the jury, "Madame de Rênal has been like a mother to me." Because he is motherless, like Stendhal himself, his profoundest desires seek some kind of maternal object. When she accedes to him, he sobs like a child. She writes her fatal letter out of what she thinks is conscience but is actually jealousy; he fires his answering shot out of what he thinks is revenge but is actually longing. Between Julien and Mathilde, the peasant's son and the peer's daughter, the tension is even stronger. Here the *devoir* is on her side; it is she, in the manner of Bernard Shaw's heroines, who finally takes the initiative. Their conversations are "animated by sentiments of the liveliest hatred." In mutual ambivalence, they fascinate and repel each other; with suspicion on both sides, they arrive at an assignation. And when they arrive at an understanding, it is based on the humiliation of her pride and the assertion of his, the masochism of the aristocrat and the sadism of the revolutionist. "Beware of that young man who has so much energy," her brother has warned her. "If the revolution starts again, he will have us all guillotined." At the ball or the opera, among the gilded youth, he cuts a sinister figure. He will be another Danton, she imagines in her proud humility, perhaps another Robespierre. When he determines to climb her balcony, we see him in his true colors: "the unhappy man at war with the whole of society."

Goethe, though he praised the psychological insight of *Le Rouge et le noir,* considered the feminine characters too romantic. They undoubtedly are, for their function is to understand Julien's true nature. It is because Julien is a romantic at heart that he, figuratively and literally, loses his head. Mathilde's cult of her beheaded ancestor, the lover of Marguérite de Valois, strengthens her for the part of a Dumas heroine, and for the macabre series of last rites that she arranges for her lover. In contrast to the naturalness of the Rênal estate at Vergy, her necrophilic love has ripened in a library, nourished on the chronicles of Brantôme and Aubigné and the novels of Rousseau and Prévost. It should not be too surprising, for those familiar with Stendhal's touchstones, that she ends by boring and irritating Julien, or that the prodigal—torn between his two mistresses, like Dimitri Karamazov between Katya and Grushenka—reverts to Madame de Rênal. It is truly surprising that Emile Faguet should accuse Stendhal of evading the issue, and propose an ending in which Julien either reaches the top of the ladder or else drags Mathilde down to his original level. If Julien had a future, it clearly would not be shared with Mathilde. She has all too clearly become, as Stendhal must have learned to say in Italy, the *terza incomoda.* So far as Stendhal's intentions are concerned, the crime is the issue, and the condemnation is the pay-off. Nothing less than complete failure will prove Julien's sincerity, vindicate his good faith, and demonstrate that he is no mere *arriviste.* Eugène de Rastignac would be too hard, Frédéric Moreau too soft, for such an act. Afterward, after Frilair has been conciliated and the jury has been fixed, Julien's fate again falls into his hands. But the trial, the sight of the assembled bourgeoisie, arouses his peculiar notion of duty. Improvising for the first time, he loads his speech with the dynamite of class consciousness. He pleads guilty to the crime of having risen in the world and pronounces his own verdict. "Gentlemen, I have not the honor of belonging to your class. You see in me a peasant who has revolted against the baseness of his fortune."

Prince Korasoff's advice to him, "Always do the opposite of what is expected of you," should have prepared us for the denouement. Julien's pent-up heroism betrays itself by one of those gusts of sensibility which cannot be foreseen by the Machiavellian calculus. Isolated in his impenitent cell, he comes to Hobbesian conclusions about the predatory human animal; he envisions society as a relentless conspiracy of power and wealth. "No, man cannot put his trust in man." Often he has naively wondered if he too were not merely another egoist, and often he has acted suspiciously like one; his last actions, at any rate, are disinterested. "The powerful idea of duty," he trusts, has saved him from living in isolation. The distinction between duty and interest, in the last analysis, is the gulf that separates the happy few from the world at large. Yet it must be admitted that the happy few fare none too happily in their pursuits; the free spirits are enchained while charlatans prosper; for those that feel, the world is a tragedy. Even Croisenois, the noble suitor of Mathilde, is killed in a duel by a millionaire named Thaler. In a world where everything else is for sale, there is one decoration that distinguishes, one honor that cannot be bought: it is the death sentence. The revolutionary Count Altamira, who has had a price set on his head, is the one character who commands Julien's wholehearted respect. Other omens foreshadow the guillotine; the news of an execution, the sound of a prisoner's song. The singer Geronimo, named for Lablache's role in *Il Matrimonio segreto,* represents those graces which are rather Italian than French. Stendhal has a way of fastening on specific details—a pair of scissors, an ancient sword, a Japanese vase—to evoke a mood or connote a situation. His most arresting metaphor is that of a tiger kept as a pet by an Englishman, who took care to keep a loaded pistol within his reach.

Though later generations of supermen and nihilists and *deracinés* and *immoralistes* pay their respects to Julien, and claim Stendhal as the founder of their *culte du moi,* no writer has more cogently insisted that egoism is self-destroying, and that the few cannot be happy when the many are unhappy. *Le Rouge et le noir,* accepted at its face value, could be made to serve as reactionary propaganda. Paul Bourget has sententiously retold the story in *Le Disciple:* his young upstart, influenced by the experimental doctrines of a philosopher modelled on Taine, seduces a young patrician and incites her to suicide. The labored moral is that new ideas are dangerous, and that the lower classes should be kept in their place. But face values are precisely what Stendhal wished to discount. "What the pride of the rich calls society" is for him a comic phenomenon; and while, in ironic footnotes, he disclaims the radical opinions of his characters, his own sympathies are with the interloper. The tragic resistance of the individual, vainly trying to uphold the integrity of his personality against the conformities and corruptions of the time, is what lends stature to Julien Sorel. At a time when it is difficult not to write satire, it is equally hard to be a hero; and Stendhal's irony fluctuates against the double standard of a realistic worldliness and romantic sensibility. Julien surrenders too early and resists too late. The desperate intelligence that guides his steps, nevertheless, is a refutation of Amiel's criticism and an assertion of freedom of the will. In Dreiser's *American Tragedy* a century later, as it happens, we see the same factors at work: bigotry and venality, the climb toward success, the compromising affair, the murderous impulse, the trial and condemnation and execution. Circumstances meanwhile have been closing in, and Clyde Griffiths is their victim. Unlike Julien, he has no elbowroom for heroics, and little responsibility for his actions. Not ideology but behaviorism offers the key to his character. The novel is no longer the confession of a mind, but has wholly become the chronicle of a milieu.

"Tender and honest" are Stendhal's adjectives for Julien, reconsidered at a distance of ten years, "ambitious, yet full of imagination and illusion." To be a lone champion of modernity, under a regimen which encouraged the shrewd and the stolid to adopt the costumes and revive the customs of the Middle Ages—surely Don Quixote was never confronted with a more preposterous situation. As for Gil Blas, that clever rogue who showed such agility in mounting to high places, what would he have made of a social hierarchy which was itself in motion, of bishops and kings who were merely invested and annointed picaroons? "O nineteenth century!" In 1823 when the radical orator, Jacques Manuel, invoked the "new energy" that had emerged with the Revolution, he was expelled from the ultra-royalist Chamber of Deputies. This was the energy, submerged again during the Restoration, that Stendhal sought to register; the heat that soon, he warned his contemporaries, would be converted into force. Temporarily it lurked behind the comic mask, the clerical uniform, the antic disposition; Julien's hypocrisy, like Hamlet's madness, was a dramatic device. French logic had frequently speculated on the paradox of the comedian: Diderot maintained that the best acting had the least feeling, while Rousseau drew tragic implications out of Molière's ridicule. From the comedy of the nineteenth century to the tragedy is a step which Julien finally takes; his superiority, which must stoop to conquer, debases itself and foregoes its conquest. The irony of ironies is that Stendhal should pattern his hero upon the classic model of the hypocrite, that sincerity should be driven to *Tartufferie.* Yet Molière's comedy, which Julien committed to memory, had a special meaning for the Restoration; it voiced a protest against the clerical regime, which could not otherwise have been heard. Even Tartuffe had his great scene, when it befell the servant to order the master out of the house. To royalty and nobility, to the clergy and the Third Estate, to the thrones and powers and dominions and vested interests, *Le Rouge et le noir* brought back that scene with all the accelerating impact of a nightmare:

> C'est à vous d'en sortir, vous qui parlex en maître:
> La maison m'appartient, je le ferai connaître.

Narrative "Uncontrol" in Stendhal

D. A. Miller

The moral desirability of closure in Jane Austen and George Eliot is inseparable from a reluctance to entertain the pleasures of narrative suspensiveness. If these pleasures are often suggested in Jane Austen, they are also thoroughly condemned. George Eliot more willingly accepts the suspensive character of narrative, but this is partly because she deeroticizes it, equating it with a state of grim process. What ensues is an anxiety at once inevitable and uninviting. Whereas Jane Austen deplores the erotics of suspensiveness, George Eliot scarcely recognizes that they exist. Accordingly, to *enjoy* being in the narrative of *Mansfield Park* is merely unprincipled, while to enjoy being in *Middlemarch* is all but impossible. Different as each novelist is in this respect, however, both exemplify the fearful attitude of the traditional novel toward its own suspensive play.

What distinguishes Stendhal from these novelists is precisely the fact that he elevates this play (in its full erotic sense) to the position of a supreme value. His consequent dislike of closure (as that which ends the possibility of play) even extends to narrative itself, insofar as it is organized in end-determined plots. Yet the traditional formal requirements of plot and ending are by no means irrelevant to Stendhal's fiction, for its cherished play is ultimately defined as the perpetually reenacted *evasion* of these requirements. Thus, Stendhal's novels must admit closural controls as part of a perverse strategy for disrupting their functioning. We can begin to explore this strategy by considering the strategist who brings it best to light, Julien Sorel.

From *Narrative and Its Discontents*. © 1981 by Princeton University Press.

THE MAN OF PLOTS

Julien Sorel is an intriguer, and his Machiavellianism has its counterpart in his paranoid readiness to detect the intrigues of others against him. Perversely enough, this sharply developed "plot sense" ought to be a useful adaptation to the terrain, for the world of Le Rouge et le noir is defined by little else than an incessant play of conspiratorial forces. Yet Julien's adaptation is strikingly dysfunctional. The paranoia is nearly always misplaced, and the progress from Verrières to Besançon to Paris depends less on Julien's actual schemes of advancement than on lateral, unforeseen developments. If the Machiavellian strategies are not very effective, it may be in part because they are executed in so careless a fashion: neglected in this or that detail, forgotten or abandoned at this or that juncture. Moreover, the moments when plots falter coincide with moments when Julien seems most closely in touch with himself, at a primary level of being. The gaffes, one beings to suspect, are slips as well: not mere inadvertencies, but—like neurotic symptoms—protests and reversions.

In an important sense, Julien's behavior in Rouge can be seen to turn on his anxious relationship to his own plots. The moment from which to start, however, is the moment of fantasy and daydream, before plot has been born.

> Dès sa première enfance, il avait eu des moments d'exaltation. Alors il songeait avec délices qu'un jour il serait présenté aux jolies femmes de Paris, il saurait attirer leur attention par quelque action d'éclat. Pourquoi ne serait-il pas aimé de l'une d'elles, comme Bonaparte, pauvre encore, avait été aimé de la brillante Mme de Beauharnais? Depuis bien des années, Julien ne passait peut-être pas une heure sans se dire que Bonaparte, lieutenant pauvre et sans fortune, s'était fait le maître du monde avec son epée. Cette idée consolait de ses malheurs qu'il croyait grands, et redoublait sa joie quand il en avait.

By treating what are in fact countless daydreams as though they were all one, Stendhal suggests the obsessive structure of recurrence that governs them. Repetition here seems to involve no difference, and although the daydream can be inserted into historical time ("from his earliest childhood," "for several years"), it apparently has no internal history of its own. Indeed, it tends to abolish the historical time in which it is constituted, by reinvoking the same atemporal state of beatitude at every replay. In addition, a logic of temporal "shortcircuiting" operates within the daydream itself. "He would be introduced to the pretty women of Paris; he would attract their attention by some brillant action." Behind so compressed a syntax would seem an attempt to convert what is inevitably a diachronic sequence into what becomes virtually a synchronic list, all of whose items are present at once. Wish and fulfillment, want and satisfaction, present and future— beginnings and ends are collapsed into copresence. "Bonaparte, an unknown lieutenant without money, made himself master of the world with his sword." Poverty and mastery, although grammatically represented as successive states, seem at a deeper level to combine in a structure of flickering alternation, such as permits *both* states to be enjoyed, as it were simultaneously. Poverty implies the mastery that will redeem it, mastery the poverty that is its stimulus. Julien's daydream might be taken as the ultimate retraction of plot, all its successive articulations drawn back (as far as grammar will allow) into an arrangement of simultaneous order: available all at once for purposes of consolation.

The daydream, therefore, is not narratable per se. Rather, narratability depends on the dissatisfaction that compels Julien to transpose his daydream into the mode of everyday reality. What awakens this dissatisfaction may simply be the obvious insubstantiality of daydreams, whose gratifications are "unreal"; but it may also be the erotic foreclosure of daydreams, whose gratifications leave nothing to be desired. In either case, it is significant that Julien comes to everyday reality with an awareness that "times have changed." In the place of an ideal past (idealized with the help of a little rouge), there has arisen a darkened state of affairs that will never permit his daydream to be directly pursued. The narratable does not, then, coincide with a naive decision to realize daydream, as it does for the characters of *Middlemarch*. More perversely, it coincides with a recognition that daydream cannot be realized—at least, not in straightforward ways. As a result, the inspiration of plot is less a longing to adequate fantasy and reality than a more devious desire to circumvent a given inadequation. Unlike Dorothea Brooke, Julien Sorel knows at the start that plot is radically different from daydream, and he aggressively assumes the difference.

> La construction de l'église et les sentences du juge de paix l'é-clairèrent tout à coup; une idée qui lui vint le rendit comme fou pendant quelques semaines, et enfin s'empara de lui avec la toute-puissance de la première idée qu'une âme passionée croit avoir inventée.
>
> "Quand Bonaparte fit parler de lui, la France avait peur d'être envahie; le mérite militaire était nécessaire et à la mode. Au-

jourd'hui, on voit des prêtres de quarante ans avoir cent mille francs d'appointements, c'est-à-dire trois fois autant que les fameux généraux de division de Napoléon. Il leur faut des gens qui leur secondent. Voilà ce juge de paix, si bonne tête, si honnête homme, jusqu'ici, si vieux, qui se déshonore par crainte de déplaire à un jeune vicaire de trente ans. Il faut être prêtre."

His project of ambition will involve certain contradictions from the first. Whereas in daydream, beginning and end were virtually copresent to enjoyment, the end is now placed at a distance to be traversed. Plot is to bring about the end, but that end is now an absence, something "to be brought about." Julien must space out the recovery of his imaginary plenitude into successive steps. Steps toward an end? or steps *from* an end? What on one face is plot's transitivity is on the other its resistance. A detour recalls the direct route. That, however, is a second problem. Is Julien's plot a detour (that is, a circuitous route of access), or is it a pure deflection? Can the black of strategy ever hope to recover a red of wish *and* fulfillment, available together and at once?

These ontological dilemmas might be appropriately reformulated in the social and historical terms provided by the novel. Julien's movement from daydream to plot can be seen to internalize the historical displacement that has overtaken France: from red to black, from the original promise of the Italian campaign ("all that [Julien] knew of history") to the construction of the imposing church in Verrières and the decisions made against the town liberals. Daydream is anachronism, and plot must involve the pathos of updating. Julien's Napoleonic urgings can only take alien and reductive forms. "J'ai gagné une bataille," he says after obtaining a three-days' leave from M. de Rênal, and the discrepancy between his language and what it actually describes is sourly comic. As for the real risks of battle, the world of *Rouge* has relocated them in the social institution of the duel, so stylized that, as Mathilde complains, "tout est su d'avance, même ce qu'on dit en tombant." Even the richly and disturbingly undermotivated attempt to kill Mme de Rênal is implicitly absorbed into the journalistic category of the *fait divers,* like the one Julien reads about in the church at Verrières (and like, of course, the article in the *Gazette des Tribunaux* from which Stendhal got his story). In a context that translates all actions into trivial parodies of the inspiration behind them, success under the Restoration becomes a monstrous deformation of an exemplary revolutionary career. Plot tends to produce its own end, which relates to the original object of desire that it was designed to reach only as black and red.

Yet the untimeliness of Julien's desire goes beyond mere anachronism, even in social-historical terms, and must ultimately be taken in something like its root sense. It is no accident that the atemporal structure of Julien's daydream takes Napoleonic themes for its content, since an essential synchrony (be it that of daydream or that of myth) governs Stendhal's treatment of the revolutionary period. Similarly, a relentlessly diachronic structure of plot—all extended arabesques of deflection and delay—orders the representation of what Stendhal might well have called Restoration comedy.

Georg Lukács has argued that the sense of history behind the historical novel—and, with a turn of the screw, behind realism itself—depended on "the French Revolution, the revolutionary wars and the rise and fall of Napoleon, which for the first time made history *a mass experience,* and moreover on a European scale" (*The Historical Novel*). The argument seems generally right, but in the case of Stendhal's novels, one wants to stand it on its head. The revolutionary verb, as it were, in Stendhal is not the insistently transitive verb of history in Lukács's sense (history as "an uninterrupted process of change"), but the essentially copulative verb of wish fulfillment and myth. In the opening chapter of *La Chartreuse de Parme*—the entry of the French into Milan in 1796 and the exemplary career of Lieutenant Robert—the historical process seems more like the stroke of a magical wand. Everything yields before this unresisted march of passion and high spirits. The Revolution would seem to have disposed of time in a spontaneous burst of energy—if only for a time. For while the revolutionary history can be written as the jubilant finale of fairy tale, contested only by token dragons, the finale of fairy tale is the beginning of novel. Much like Emma's "perfect union" in Jane Austen or St. Theresa's "rapturous consciousness" in George Eliot, the Revolution in Stendhal intrinsically *has no story.* For the most part, it is scattered across his texts in fragments of memory, or myth, or daydream—taken up directly only when, as in the *Chartreuse,* it is about to be over. The real motivation of his fiction (in the sense given to the word by the Russian Formalists) lies elsewhere, in the black plots of reaction. It is in the court intrigues of Parma, the electoral campaign of *Lucien Leuwen,* Julien's mission to Strasbourg, and the like, that the novels most pointedly thematize the fact of narrative. In almost a strictly formal sense, Stendhal's novels *must* begin at Waterloo or some version of it, for as he sees it, the essence of revolutionary history can scarcely be narrated at all.

Thus, two modalities of deviation appropriate Julien's daydream at the moment it becomes plot ("il faut être prêtre"): an ontological one, spacing out fulfillment in time and consigning it to incompleteness at any given point; and a social-ideological one, recasting daydream into its own non-convertible terms. Together they determine the drama of what Sartre has called "counterfinality": the deflection of the project by the very instruments it must employ. The "terminal objectification," to use Sartre's terms, will not correspond to the "original choice" ("Question de méthode")—the end arrived at will no longer be the end that one wanted to reach. A local and easily isolated example of such counterfinality might be found in the un-announced nocturnal visit that Julien pays to Mme de Rênal after his de-parture from the seminary. A fresh convert to the religion of remorse, she resists his advances and so sharpens their edge. Unhappily, Julien becomes a strategist ("un froid politique"), and recounts his experience in the sem-inary in such a way as to exploit her pity. As his "last resource," he resolutely informs her that he is now off to Paris.

> —Oui, madame, je vous quitte pour toujours, soyez heureuse; adieu.
> Il fit quelques pas vers la fenêtre; déjà il l'ouvrait. Mme de Rênal s'élança vers lui et se précipita dans ses bras.
> Ainsi, après trois heures de dialogue, Julien obtint ce qu'il avait désiré avec tant de passion pendant les deux premières. Un peu plus tòt arrivés, le retour aux sentiments tendres, l'éclipse des remords chez Mme de Rênal eussent eté un bonheur divin; ainsi obtenus avec art, ce ne fut plus qu'un plaisir.

In such a framework, one needs to place Julien's curiously patchy performances. The irruption of his "passion intérieure" into his schemes forms part of an unconscious enterprise of nostalgia: a series of attempts to inscribe the full promise of daydream within the plot that frustrates it. No sooner is Julien's plot formed than it is betrayed:

> Une fois, au milieu de sa nouvelle piété, il y avait déjà deux ans que Julien étudiait la théologie, il fut trahi par une irruption soudaine du feu qui dévorait son âme. Ce fut chez M. Chelan, à un diner de prêtres auquel le bon curé l'avait présenté comme un prodige d'instruction, il lui arriva de louer Napoléon avec fureur.

Stendhal's passive constructions ("il fut trahi," "il lui arriva de parler") make it clear that Julien is not in full control of such lapses. Whether against his will or simply without his willing, the coherence of the scenario of ambition is undermined by a regressive fondness for "souvenirs" of archaic passion. Imprudently, Julien keeps now a portrait of Napoleon under his mattress, now the address of a friendly café waitress in his trunk. All at once, he decides to see Mme de Rênal a last time before leaving for Paris. In Paris, he makes a pilgrimage to Malmaison and to the tomb of Marshal Ney; in London, he visits the imprisoned radical Philip Vane. At an embassy reception in England, he can't help saying that "there are three hundred thousand young Frenchmen of twenty-five who passionately want war," and at the ball of M. de Retz, he can't stop talking to the exiled republican Altamira.

Julien's most conspicuous lapse, surely, is his decision to "avenge" himself on Mme de Rênal—because she has maligned him in a letter to the Marquis de la Mole, who as a result has repudiated him. Perhaps, as Mathilde theatrically takes to saying, "all is lost"; but then again, perhaps not. Is the marquis's anger as final and irrevocable as he seeks to make it and his daughter to interpret it? Some doubt would seem at least permitted, for the marquis has been already and more than once displeased with Julien's conquest of Mathilde (on grounds, moreover, similar to those furnished in Mme de Rênal's letter), and he has each time moderated his displeasure. On the other hand, it is a certainty that the marquis will never "come round" after a murder; then, all will be lost indeed. From the standpoint of Julien's ambition, no move could be more unwise than his attempt to shoot his former mistress. Yet the initial shock of the marquis's fury reaches him, paradoxically, "in the midst of transports of the most unbridled ambition." At the very moment when he would seem most committed to the spoils of ambition, he perversely acts to despoil himself.

One might recall, however, that Julien has himself solicited Mme de Rênal's letter. The marquis writes in uncomprehending rage, "L'impudent m'avait engagé lui-même à écrire à Mme de Rênal." It is as though Julien unconsciously sought in the letter another "souvenir": a disguised remembrance of a love whose value has seemed to increase with the distance of retrospection from which it is viewed. Yet even souvenirs, it would now appear, have changed color.

> Pauvre et avide, c'est à l'aide de l'hypocrisie la plus consommée, et par la séduction d'une femme faible et malheureuse, que cet homme a cherché à se faire un état et à devenir quelque chose. C'est une partie de mon pénible devoir d'ajouter que je suis obligée de croire que M. J. . . . n'a aucun principe de religion. En conscience, je suis contrainte de penser qu'un de ses moyens pour réussir dans une maison, est de chercher à séduire la femme qui a le principal crédit. Couvert par une apparence de désin-

téressement et par des phrases de roman, son grand et unique
objet est de parvenir à disposer du maître de la maison et de sa
fortune.

In an obvious sense, the letter is grossly unfair, even to the point of ex-
aggerating Julien's tactical abilities. "The most consummate hypocrisy:
seems an extravagant formula with which to designate the naive, clumsily
enforced bluffing that went into the seduction of Mme de Rênal and Mathilde. Yet if the letter is not true in the sense of conforming to the full
portrait of Julien drawn by the novel, it just fits the facts and it offers a
different way in which these facts might be seen. Muddle is erected into
system, and incidental effects treated as manifest intentions. The letter's
reductiveness drains Julien's career of his own particular relationship to it,
and so confers on it all the coherence that his depth of feeling had tended
to disperse. By significant omission, the letter brings into question the very
existence of such feeling. This is a souvenir that refuses to function as such.
It says, in effect, that the event to which it testifies never really happened—
Julien has never been there.

His attempt to destroy Mme de Rênal, then, is an extreme attempt to
save what she has meant to him—to put her back in her place at the dead
center of red. At the same time, it forcefully rejects the spirit of the letter,
adding a new fact to the biography that the readings of hypocrisy and
ambition cannot well account for. Most important, this unlawful act (in a
double sense: both against the law and against the rules of his own game)
brings about the final reunion of Julien and Mme de Rênal, a reunion
invested with the only values that now matter. Under their pressure, Julien
dismisses his past plotting as an irrelevant diversion, and with it much of
the novel. Even the issues of his long-tortured examination of conscience
(sincerity, immortality, and the like) give way to the cry: "Grand Dieu,
Dieu bon, Dieu indulgent, rends-moi celle que j'aime!"

Figure has yielded decisively to ground, as Julien's attention redirects
itself from ambition to love, and authority passes from the official performance to an affecting drama of wholly different priorities occurring in the
wings. Only in the blinds of his official project, in its failure to be totally
absorbing, does Julien now place the worthwhile meanings of his life. The
reader, however, has been encouraged to reach such a conclusion long before
Julien. Julien has practiced figure-ground reversals from the very beginning
(although without surrendering to their full implications), and it is on these
that Stendhal has founded his case for Julien's superior worth. The many
moments in which a project is suspended, and the energies sustaining it

released in irrelevant or even subversive affect, are his moments of greatest moral value and novelistic richness. Conversely, at rare moments when Julien attends wholly to the demands of plot, he seems both morally contemptible and novelistically flat, no different from all the other vicious puppets that people the world of *Rouge*.

An obvious pair of examples, one a plot-breaking lapse, the other a plot-conforming surrender, concerns the "dépôt de mendicité. When M. Valenod silences the singing in the poorhouse (which shares a wall with his dining room), it is "too much for Julien."

> Il avait les manières, mais non pas encore le coeur de son état. Malgré toute son hypocrisie si souvent exercée, il sentit une grosse larme couler le long de sa joue.
>
> Il essaya de la cacher avec le verre vert, mais il lui fut absolument impossible de faire honneur au vin du Rhin. *L'empêcher de chanter!* se disait-il à lui-même, ô mon Dieu! et tu le souffres!
>
> Par bonheur, personne ne remarqua son attendrissement de mauvais ton. Le percepteur des contributions avait entonné une chanson royaliste. Pendant le tapage du refrain, chanté en choeur: Voilà donc, se disait la conscience de Julien, la sale fortune à laquelle tu parviendras, et tu n'en jouiras qu'à cette condition et en pareille compagnie! Tu auras peut-être une place de vingt mille francs, mais il faudra que, pendant que tu te gorges de viandes, tu empêches de chanter le pauvre prissonier; tu donneras à diner avec l'argent que tu auras volé sur sa misérable pitance, et pendant ton dîner il sera encore plus malheureux!—O Napoléon! qu'il était doux de ton temps de monter à la fortune par les dangers d'une bataille; mais augmenter lâchement la douleur du misérable!

Later, however, confronted with Valenod's appalling success, he requests the direction of this same poorhouse for his father:

> —A la bonne heure, dit le marquis en reprenant l'air gai; accordé; je m'attendais à des moralités. Vous vous formez.
>
> M. de Valenod apprit à Julien que le titulaire du bureau de loterie de Verrières venait de mourir: Julien trouva plaisant de donner cette place à M. de Cholin, ce vieil imbécile dont jadis il avait ramassé la pétition dans la chambre de M. de la Mole. Le marquis rit de bien bon coeur de la pétition que Julien récita en lui faisant signer la lettre qui demandait cette place au ministre des finances.

A peine M. de Cholin nommé, Julien apprit que cette place avait été demandée par la députation du département pour M. Gros, le célèbre géomètre: cette homme généreux n'avait que quatorze cents francs de rente, et chaque année prêtait six cents francs au titulaire qui venait de mourir, pour l'aider à élever sa famille.

The important recognition that Julien achieves in the earlier scene at the Valenods is pointedly sacrificed in the later one at the Hôtel de la Mole. Now the demands of Machiavellianism are unhesitatingly met and begin to seem like positive gratifications. (Even here, perhaps, one might see hidden messages of dissent transmitted in the very conduct of compliance— and hence, a wider interval between Julien and his role that can appear on the surface. For if he now accepts what the poorhouse stands for, it is also the case that he accepts it for his father, whom he hates, as if to suggest privately that it were only fit for such a one. Moreover, to assign the lottery bureau to an acknowledged fool may be a personal comment on a system in which assignments seem no less perversely motivated. Julien's cynical amusement would then be only the guilt of an accomplice assuaging itself.) Whatever qualifications we may want to introduce, it is nevertheless clear that his response in the first episode defines something like Julien's authentic self, a residual worth as yet unadjusted to the requirements of his social career; and that what the marquis sees as Julien's formation indicates only the extent to which he has been deformed.

Implicitly, my discussion has so far remained within what might be called the novel's official view of itself. I have seen plot in *Rouge* much as Julien comes to see it: as a pure counterfinality, delaying and deflecting fulfillment, threatening to absorb the self into its own graceless arabesques. There seems no mistaking Stendhal's official antithesis, whatever names one prefers to give the opposing terms: on the one hand, the passionate condensation of daydream, which he likes, and on the other, the postponement and aberration of plot, which he regrets. To an important extent, *Rouge* is a novel about the dilemmas of romanticism, with a demonstrable romantic bias in its own presentation of them.

As such, it is well described by theories of the novel that (albeit in chastened form) reconstitute this opposition and share these valorizations. *Rouge* may be meaningfully read according to the schema provided in Lukács's *Theory of the Novel:* as a nostalgic quest for a coincidence of life and essence, frustrated (or at least problematized) by a world that holds them separate. Similarly, it may also be seen to embody the related structure elaborated by Lucien Goldmann—an anachronistic hero harkens back to a world in which unmediated value ("use value") was the dominant form of moral economy (*Pour une sociologie du roman*). My own discussion has been an attempt to give specific content to precisely this anachronistic movement of nostalgia. Nostalgia implies that there was a home where . . . (in the epic world); anachronism, that there was a time when . . . (in a precapitalistic economy). Both are treated as holdovers from an original state of affairs; and as a result, either tends to seem authentic in ways that what frustrates it is not. At an obvious level, *Rouge* is organized along these lines. Stendhal's portrayal of the Napoleonic period presents a home par excellence, and Julien is evidently a character who has been born at the wrong time.

Suppose, however, that instead of placing the source of the nostalgia outside a system that "then" appropriates it, one sees *both* the nostalgia *and* what is perceived to threaten it interlocking in the play of a single system. Suppose one sees anachronism as a complementary version of modernity, in the same contemporary structure. Suppose, finally, one begins to recognize how dependent Stendhal's romantic bias is for its expression on what allegedly thwarts it. Figure and ground, after all, dovetail into a single gestalt; and if plot foils daydream, might it not also act as a foil for it? be its very condition of possibility? Might not both the values of individualism and the threats to it, rather than succeeding one another (as romantic myth would have it), be contemporaneous, mutually dependent discoveries (as it would seem historically the case)?

Some such recognition would seem to operate practically in *Rouge,* if mainly under cover. A chief example might be Julien's seduction of Mme de Rênal. Even here, of course, it is possible to treat the scene as part of a problematic of sheer counterfinality. From Julien's point of view, counterfinality involves the deflection of the end by the means. "Qui veut la fin veut les moyens," he will say later to Count Altamira, in good Machiavellian style; but here the means seem to produce their own end, different from the one presumably desired. Strategy has evidently absorbed so much passion that none remains for pleasure. The paramilitary means of seduction have obtained—only a paramilitary seduction. The moment of *bonheur* is literally left blank in the text—or, to put it in the novel's own color scheme, it has been entirely blacked out. Only when Julien forgets his role, on the following nights, can he begin to enjoy himself.

From the reader's point of view, counterfinality appears in its complementary form, as what might be called "counterinstrumentality." The desired end has been brought about by means different from those that were supposed to obtain it. When Mme de Rênal scolds Julien, who has boldly entered her bedroom, he quite simply bursts into tears. Tellingly, these unscheduled tears lubricate his victory: "Quelques heures après, quand Julien sortit de la chambre de Mme de Rênal, on eût pu dire, en style de roman, qu'il n'avait plus rien à désirer." Indeed, victory has been largely owing to the love Julien had already inspired ("qu'il *avait* inspiré"—my italics), and to the unexpected impression made on him by feminine charms rather than to his maladroit shrewdness. Strategy would hardly have worked if unaccompanied by a redeeming counterpoint in the unguarded, the impetuous, the unforeseen.

Either way one takes it, plot would seem mainly a futile enterprise. For Julien, whose plot has failed to produce a love experience, the end has been deflected by the means. For Mme de Rênal, who is initiated by Julien's seduction into an experience of genuine passion, the end has been reached by means other than those meant to promote it. Plot either misses its mark of necessity, or hits it by accident. Yet running counter to these typically Stendhalian ironies is a rather different possibility:

> Mon Dieu! être heureux, être aimé, n'est-ce que ça? Telle fut la première pensée de Julien, en rentrant dans sa chambre. Il était dans cet état d'étonnement et de trouble inquiet où tombe l'âme qui vient d'obtenir ce qu'elle a longtemps désiré. Elle est habituée à désirer, ne trouve plus quoi désirer, et cependant n'a pas encore de souvenirs.

What matters to the narrator here is not the "arrival" of fulfillment, but the "journey" of desire: the movement of traversing a distance, which constitutes desire and reconstitutes it at every turn in the road. On the one hand, plot has been seen as the consignment of fulfillment to a succession of steps and to socially given forms of alienation. Rupture, reversal, retraction were strategies whereby to escape from plot into a wholeness of fulfillment. Here, on the other hand, that wholeness is very nearly empty, and that same temporal and social adjournment of fulfillment comes to seem almost relished for the sheer charge that it confers on desire.

Very basically, it becomes a problem of having and eating one's cake. Without exactly resolving the contradiction, Julien develops an undeclared tactic of transaction that permits him to pass from one side of it to the other, in the manner of a Sartrian *tourniquet*. We might describe the *tourniquet* in the following way. Desire treats middles as anticipations of the end; and it puts ends back into a middle, by forgetting or revising their status as ends. Ending can be accepted only as prolepsis; when it is met in its proper position (at the end!), the sequence needs to be extended to eclipse its closural finality. So, the edge of Julien's desire will be restored once his affair has become a memory, for ends remembered are already in the middle of something else.

Julien's curiously undaunted naiveté depends critically on a need to keep himself in a state of surprise; *"le besoin d'anxiété,"* as an epigraph in *Rough* puts it, apparently referring to Mathilde but implicating as well Julien himself. The way in which anxiety works turns on the felt proximity of an ending. When an ending is sensed to be all too far removed, Julien is tempted to enjoy it in advance, borrowing against vague future expectations. Typically, this takes the form of a plot-breaking gaffe. When an ending is at hand, however, he seems to regret the fact, and to try to deprive the finale of its finality and so restore to it some of the distance of approach. The weird and pathological game that Julien and Mathilde play together might stand as an almost perfectly realized figure of a plot with a continually repostponed end point. As soon as Julien reaches the point where he can be natural, he meets afresh the need to use artifice, the end functioning merely to relay a cycle of repetitions.

In this perspective, one must return to the scene of the crime, which now becomes explicable in yet another sense. Immediately before the "thunderstorm" brought about by Mme de Rênal's letter, Julien faces the fact that he has virtually achieved the objects of his ambition:

> Le soir, lorsqu[e Mathilde] apprit à Julien qu'il était lieutenant de hussards, sa joie fut sans bornes. On peut se la figurer par l'ambition de toute sa vie, et par la passion qu'il avait maintenant pour son fils. Le changement de nom le frappait d'étonnement.
>
> Après tout, pensait-il, mon roman est fini, et à moi seul tout le mérite. J'ai su me faire aimer de ce monstre d'orgueil, ajoutait-il en regardant Mathilde; son père ne peut vivre sans elle et elle sans moi.

Yet although he recognizes "the end of his novel," Julien's tone is far from one of restored equilibrium. His sadistic dominance seems too desperately asserted to be assured. It is almost as though Julien couldn't think of closure without creating new enclaves of narratable tension. Placed in such a context, Mme de Rênal's letter would become an unadmitted blessing in disguise, offering a spectacular occasion *not to terminate,* to spin out the plot still further. There is no place for a *telos* in Julien's surprise tactics; there are only displacements of it. A sliding *telos* allows plot always to anticipate its ending but never to attain it—to thicken, one might say, but not to congeal. Plot is thus kept in an effectively permanent state of irresolution.

At the same time, this attempt to displace the end becomes ultimately part of an attempt to make it absolute. Julien has refused one form of closure only to be confronted at last with another, death being the inalienable ending par excellence. To the extent that Julien's crime, his defense plea at the trial, and his behavior afterward contribute to "une sorte de suicide," they are efforts to establish an ending that cannot be cheated, and will end the very process of cheating.

Yet even here, under sentence of death, the anxiety of coming to an end continues and at a raised pitch. There is now an absolute ending, but what is the sequence that it can be said to end? What does death conclude? "Life" is an inadequate answer, for Julien's death scarcely comes as an appropriate biological ending (to an internally coherent sequence of birth, maturity, decay). It closes the biological series but is not itself produced by it. Of what is it the ending? in what series does it belong? Most simply, one might take death as concluding a sequence of crime and punishment; but one would still be left with the gap between them, after the one and before the other.

Occurring precisely in the gap of this *temps mort* is Julien's extended and fragmented prison soliloquy. Significantly, it enacts a meditation on modes of meeting the end, not as an arbitrary end point, but as an appropriate closure. Julien would want to personalize death as *his* death. "On meurt comme on peut; *moi je ne veux penser à la mort qu'à ma manière.* Que m'importent *les autres?* Mes relations avec *les autres* vont être tranchées brusquement" (first italics mine). More or less explicitly, his soliloquy attempts to prepare him for death—better put, prepare death for him. The conclusion must be made natural, internally motivated, the capstone of a meaning. Thus, under the pressure of death, Julien elaborates a philosophy meant to make him desire its coming ("de nature à faire désirer la mort") by disgusting him with things human. For example, "J'ai aimé la vérité. . . . Où est-elle? . . . Partout hypocrisie, ou du moins charlatanisme, même chez les plus vertueux, même chez le plus grands; et ses lèvres prirent l'expression du dégoût. . . . Non, l'homme ne peut pas se fier à l'homme."

René Girard has called this reevaluation, in which "Julien disavows his will to power" and "breaks away from the world which fascinated him," his "conversion in death" (*Deceit, Desire, and the Novel*). Yet it is hard to see Julien renouncing his "will to power," when his conversion is basically an attempt to *master* death, to make it a choice. Conversion is a way to inscribe the life and death opposition within life, and the death that it mimes gives a purchase on the real thing. Julien dies to his old self (to use a familiar formula for conversion), so that his actual death can do no more to him than he has already done to himself. Conversion naturalizes death, and conversely, death sanctions the validity of conversion—it makes the before and after dichotomy imposed by conversion less problematic, if only because there will not be much "after" to undermine its neatness.

Despite the device of a conversion, Julien is still unable to meet his death directly. Without engaging the Sartrian ontology en bloc, one might introduce here Sartre's argument in *L'Etre et le néant* about the impossibility of living toward one's death:

> Loin que le mort soit ma possibilité propre, elle est *un fait contingent* qui, en tant que tel, m'échappe par principe et resortit originellement à ma facticité. Je ne saurais ni découvrir ma mort, ni l'attendre, ni prendre une attitude envers elle, car elle est ce qui se révèle comme l'indécouvrable, ce qui désarme toutes les attentes, ce qui glisse dans toutes les attitudes et particulièrement dans celles qu'on prendrait vis-à-vis d'elle, pour les transformer en conduites extériorisées et figées dont le sens est pour toujours confié à d'autres qu'à nous-mêmes. La mort est un pur fait, comme la naissance; elle vient à nous du dehors et elle nous transforme en dehors.

Much as in Freud the dream can never say no, the Sartrian project can never say die. *Avant la lettre,* Julien makes Sartre's point in explicitly grammatical terms, when he remembers an observation of Danton's: "C'est singulier, le verbe guillotiner ne peut pas se conjuguer dans tous ses temps; on peut bien dire: Je serai guillotiné, tu seras guillotiné, mais on ne dit pas: J'ai été guillotiné." A subject can never grasp his own death, because grammatically he can never "say" it. "I" cannot be the grammatical subject of a proposition that logically presupposes the abolition of the subjectivity that an "I" constitutes.

Thus, what seems a movement toward the end turns out necessarily to be a flight from it. The philosophy that "makes death desired" in fact continually elides the fact of death, whether its reflections turn toward an afterlife, toward Mme de Rênal in this life, or toward both at once, as in the following deflected syllogism:

> Ainsi la mort, la vie, l'éternité, choses fort simples pour qui aurait les organes assez vastes pour les concevoir. . . .

> Une mouche éphémère nâit à neuf heures du matin dans les
> grands jours d'été, pour mourir à cinq heures du soir; comment
> comprendrait-elle le mot *nuit?*
>
> Donnez-lui cinq heures d'existence de plus, elle voit et com-
> prend ce que c'est que la nuit.
>
> Ainsi moi, je mourrai à 23 ans. Donnez-moi cinq années de
> vie de plus, pour vivre avec Mme de Rênal.
>
> Et il se mit à rire comme Méphistophélès. Quelle foli de dis-
> cuter ces grands problèms!

Inevitably, Julien's thoughts slip back into retrospect, or forward into plans
and prophecy. Mathilde must marry the Marquis de Croisenois, or later,
when he is killed, M. de Luz; she will neglect his child; Mme de Rênal
must promise to care for it; and so on.

"What do *the others* matter to me?" Julien's anxiety stems from a perfectly correct sense that they matter a great deal—that finally they will be
all that matters. For, in a proper Sartrian manner, the meaning of his life
proves not to be in his control. Stendhal has already shown how the sugges-
tively undermotivated force of Julien's crime is made instantly subject to a
series of social appropriations: for the Abbé de Frilair, it means a chance at
a bishopric; for the jurors, an occasion for class spite, for the town ladies,
an invitation to sentimental indulgence; for the vigilant priest, an oppor-
tunity to make reputation; for the hawkers, a salable commodity. (Moreover, if we have understood the point of the demonstration, there is every
reason to extend the sequence: for the newspapers, some hot copy; for a
novelist, a fascinating subject.) Julien's horror that "at every moment [the
priest] is repeating my name" speaks for itself. Even while alive, Julien has
become public property; death will complete the process, and its meaning
can *only* be conferred by "the others." Hence Julien's anxious attention to
the scenario that Mathilde and Mme de Rênal must follow on his death;
hence also, his wish for posthumous developments that might revise the
public meaning of his life. Both come together, significantly, in a concern
for his son:

> —La mort de mon fils serait au fond un bonheur pour l'orgueil
> de votre famille [de la Mole], c'est ce que devineront les subal-
> ternes. La negligence sera le lot de cet enfant du malheur et de
> la honte. . . . J'espère qu'à une époque que je ne veux point
> fixer, mais que pourtant mon courage entrevoit, vous obéirez à
> mes dernières recommandations: Vous épouserez M. le Marquis
> de Croisenois.

—Quoi, déshonorée!

—Le déshonneur ne pourra prendre sur un nom tel que le votre. Vous serez une veuve et la veuve d'un fou, voilà tout. J'irai plus loin: mon crime n'ayant point l'argent pour moteur ne sera point déshonorant. Peut-être à cette époque, quelque législateur philosophe aura obtenu, des préjugés de ses contemporains, la suppression de la peine de mort. Alors, quelque voix amie dira comme un exemple: Tenez, le premier époux de Mlle de la Mole était un fou, mais non pas un méchant homme, un scélérat. Il fut absurde de faire tomber cette tête. . . . Alors ma mémoire ne sera point infâme; du moins après un certain temps.

The possibilities that Julien elaborates and even tries to manage are, of course, indefinitely postponed by the novel. Whom does Mathilde marry? Does she marry at all? Does she eventually look back on her episode with Julien with embarrassment, as he predicts? What happens to their son, whose appointed guardian dies before he is born? It may be futile to speculate along the lines of such questions, but it is a matter of some importance to recognize that they cannot be answered, especially since far more basic questions are kept in a similar state of suspension. "Serais-je un méchant?" Julien asks himself in prison. Although the fact that he is now able to pose such a question does not go without its moral evaluation, the question itself raises a serious problem of interpretation. If one treats it as a mainly rhetorical question—that is, meant as such in the light of the reader's superior knowledge—Julien's soliloquy gets reduced to a piece of sentimentality, in the manner of Dickens. (The scruples that Amy Dorrit or Florence Dombey entertain about their conduct never seriously indict it, but only invite us to feel sorry for them.) On the other hand, if one takes it as a legitimate question, whose answer is not already given, then one must acknowledge that it goes unanswered—or rather, that there is evidence for either way of answering it. "Ai-je beaucoup aimé?" is another question, presenting a similar problem. Much in our interpretation of *Rouge* would seem to hang on how we answer it, and yet it appears that we aren't allowed to answer it at all.

One is brought back (as one always must be) to the crime, the most crucial example of the text's own foul play. The examples so far given might easily be explained as part of a novelistic attempt to specify the complex density of experience, always throwing up questions that conspicuously fail to grasp its real intricacy. The interpretation of Julien's crime, however, necessarily stands in the position of keystone to any interpretation of the novel. It simply must be explained; for if it is "inexplicable" (as the Abbé de Frilair and Julien's Jansenist confessor both say it is), then so is Julien himself, and so to an important extent is *Le Rouge et le noir*. His crime is the most spectacular and consequential act of self-definition that Julien performs, but perversely, the scene of the crime is the chief locus of the text's indeterminacy. One is forced to wonder whether, at the level of interpretation, the crime be only a figure for this, the real transgression: the signifying act par excellence has no decisively apparent signified.

Julien himself seems in some doubt about why he did it. "Je me suis vengé" is his first statement of motive, and this by itself would have seemed plain enough, although why he *decided* to avenge himself—moreover, in so self-punishing a way—might still have remained a puzzle. Other theories of motivation, however, are also broached. In his defense plea, for instance, Julien implies that the frustrations of class have been an important source of motive. Furthermore, after the trial, he tells himself: "enfin j'ai voulu la tuer par ambition ou par amour de Mathilde." Ambition? It is hard to see a public homicide as an act of ambition. Love for Mathilde? when he will tell Mme de Rênal a little later "I have loved only you"? The Abbé de Frilair seems at one point to suggest that the crime was motivated by jealousy—"why else would M. Sorel have chosen the church, if not for the reason that precisely there, at that moment, his rival was celebrating the mass?"—and Mme de Rênal offers to say as much to the king. Does she believe it? For as one critic has rightly seen, there is indeed a sense in which Julien may be motivated by jealousy—"jealousy, perhaps, at the tone of those religious phrases [in Mme de Rênal's letter], remembering that if Napoleon was Mme de Rênal's rival, the church was his" (Michael Wood, *Stendhal*).

One cannot then agree with Gérard Genette that Stendhal leaves Julien's crime unmotivated, in order to confer on it "by his refusal of all explanation, the wild individuality that characterizes the unforeseeability of great actions" ("Vraisemblance et motivation," *Figures II*). To assert simply that Julien's act is unintelligible, a signifier without a signified, seems at the very least to underplay the speculation about motive and intention that occurs in the novel. The fact that a novelist doesn't explicitly offer a motive may not mean that there is none to derive. What Genette calls an "ellipsis of intention" may often function practically as a kind of understatement in the text, the reader being encouraged to infer what is not directly stated. (Genette, of course, recognizes this kind of ellipsis-litotes, but he restricts its occurrence to highly conventionalized genre literature, in which the code is too obvious to need specification.) Indeed, Genette treats Stendhal's so-

called refusal of all explanation in exactly this way. The lack of an explanation is instantly converted into an implied explanation of a second order:
the uniqueness—Genette might say the codelessness—of a great action.
The possibility of meaning is barely threatened. The great refusal is no
sooner posed than recouped in a familiar Stendhalian thematic of the *être
supérieur*. Once this has been done, one could quite easily group Julien's
inexplicable crime with those highly explicable acts of twentieth-century
French literature: Lafcadio's "gratuitous" act in Gide, and Mathieu's "free"
act in Sartre's *La Mort dans l'âme*.

In fact, of course, the text offers a superabundance of psychological
explanations—venegeance, ambition, love for Mathilde, jealousy—and this
is to ignore what other motives might result from the ingenuity of critical
inference. If anything, Julien's crime is overdetermined. Yet each separate
motive on its own merits is insufficient, and all the motives taken together
do not command a cohesive psychological case. Genette is right to say that
the crime has no obviously given signified, but he fails to recognize how
Stendhal makes us pass from one possible signified to another. Motivation
is not open a priori; it is only *left open,* finally, when the process of interpretation is exhausted and suspends itself, as it were, in marks of ellipsis.
That process makes us aware not of an absence of meaning (quickly translated into the idiosyncrasy of the *être supérieur*), but of a suspension of
meaning: its continual postponement to a tomorrow that never comes. Any
attempt to discuss the crime implicitly recognizes this deferment, at least
insofar as it is this lack of an immediately given meaning that makes discussion possible in the first place.

In my own analysis, I have suggested two ways in which the crime
might be read: as plot renounced and as plot prolonged. Yet while each
explanation seemed required by its own series of moments in the text, both
explanations taken together are plainly contradictory. This fact might now
be seen to define the explosive force of the act itself. Unlike other actions,
which took place *within a tourniquet* of desire, this act wholly contains the
tourniquet: it *is* its separate and contradictory moments in one. As such,
might not Julien's crime be a parable of the *tourniquet* of interpretation that
it initiates? We center our readings of *Rouge* on the crime, and then find
that we cannot give our center a decisive content. We privilege this moment
in the text as a moment of all-presence ("everything is here," as we like to
say); but as we endeavor to make our center more than a merely formal
one, we must succumb to what Roland Barthes calls "the enchantment of
the signifier" (*S/Z*). A formal promise and a practical disappointment make
up a vicious circle.

The Promise

Julien's crime necessarily focuses any reading of *Rouge*, superseding the ordinary novelistic deployment of incident and character in order to gesture toward an overriding revelation of destiny. This is so because the novel builds up to the crime—that is, it has set up a pattern of expectations, which the crime can be seen to complete. Early in the novel, for instance, Julien finds in the church at Verrières a newspaper account of the "execution and last moments of Louis Jenrel, executed at Besançon." If Julien only half-recognizes the anagram, the reader is likely to be embarrassed by the use of so obvious a device on the part of so sophisticated a novelist. (Other embarrassments of this sort in nineteenth-century fiction, of course, are not wanting—Anna Karenina's dream, Mrs. Tulliver's fears that Maggie will "tumble in" the Floss and "get drowned," Tess Durbeyfield's "prefigurative superstitions," and so on.) There are other hints about Julien's destiny as well, most notably Mathilde's piece of wit that "only sentence of death distinguishes a man; it's the only thing that can't be bought." One can deplore such crudity, or more loyally, one can say that Stendhal couldn't really have meant it; but it is best to take such heavy-handed hinting for what it is: a way to center the fiction and to guarantee its meaning.

These emphatic prolepses are only the most conspicuous aspect of what Barthes has generally called the "completeness" ("la complétude") of the traditional text. "Terms and their connections are posed (invented) in such a way as to join one another, double one another, create an illusion of continuity. Fullness generates the pattern which is supposed to 'express' it, and the pattern calls forth its complement, its coloring." This completeness can also be seen as a sort of redundancy, a superfluity of signification, imposing "a dense fullness of meaning . . . a kind of semantic chatter, proper to the archaic or infantile era of modern discourse, marked by the obsessive fear of failing to communicate." Barthes here would call attention to the way in which meaning in the traditional novel depends on *matching up:* answer is matched up with question, fulfillment with prophecy, end with beginning. As part of its pretension to a mastery of meaning (Barthes's "maîtrise du sens"), the traditional novel is set up like a somewhat scrambled catechism: a system of interrogations and responses that legitimize one another.

In this way, *Rouge* points to its own key as such. The echoes of prolepsis appear to have been called forth in advance by an originating voice. Here, the novel would say, in the crime, is the plenum of meaning available elsewhere in the text only in dispersed fragments. The reader finds himself miming Julien's retreat from plot (temporality and syntax) to a daydream-like moment in which everything would be present at once. For on the level of reading, the crime is the novel's transcendent precipitate, much like daydream on the level of story. It haunts, directing and deflecting, whatever sequence we might establish to grasp the novel's meaning. It is the souvenir that we must always keep in mind.

The Disappointment

Carrying within it its preliminaries and its consequences, the crime is formally announced as the scene of all-presence; yet interpretation of the crime is explicitly invited, as though this scene of presence needed to be supplemented and completed by a meaning that we must seek to find. As I have already argued, however, every meaning that one is tempted to apply seems incomplete, and one moves from one temptation to another finally (only finally) to suspend the process. Shifting explanations from one teasing suggestion to another, one engages in the process of deferring Julien's knowability. Once more, the reader reenacts a gesture of the protagonist—this time, his gesture of prolongation. One is never allowed to reach the end of interpretation, much as Julien's psychology can never constitute its own annihilation.

The Vicious Circle

The crime anchors the play of meanings in the text, but we are left at sea about the nature of the anchor—always drifting, always restrained by its tug. Julien's act of violence formally puts an end to our anxiety about meaning by giving meaning a location. It also, however, dooms this anxiety to repeat itself in an endless series—endless for the reason that (as Freud said about the quest for irreplaceable objects) "every surrogate . . . fails to provide the desired satisfaction" ("A Special Type of Choice of Object Made by Men"). We are set looking, precisely, for an irreplaceable object, the meaning that will regulate and control the novel's production of meaning, and we know the place where this meaning is to be found. Yet we find that anything we put in this place is already a replacement, never meeting the demands made on it by its station.

The Novel and the Guillotine, or Fathers and Sons in *Le Rouge et le noir*

Peter Brooks

Le Rouge et le noir offers an exemplary entry into the nineteenth-century novel, its dynamics, and the interpretive problems these pose. Published a few months after the triumph of the bourgeoisie in the Revolution of 1830—inaugurating an era of expansive capitalism and the acceleration of social change—*Le Rouge et le noir* displays an unprecedented concern with energy—the hero's and the text's—and provides a first decisive representation of man constructing his own life's plot in response to the sociopolitical dynamics of modern history, which both shapes the individual career and plays roulette with its most concerted plans. As Harry Levin has written, with Stendhal we undergo "the rites of initiation into the nineteenth century," and this is so in good part because Stendhal's novels are inescapably pervaded by a historical perspective that provides an interpretive framework for all actions, ambitions, self-conceptions, and desires (*The Gates of Horn*). Nowhere is the historical problematic more evident than in the question of authority that haunts *Le Rouge et le noir,* not only in the minds of its individual figures but in its very narrative structures. The novel not only represents but also is structured by an underlying warfare of legitimacy and usurpation; it hinges on the fundamental question, to whom does France belong? This question in turn implicates and is implicated in an issue of obsessive importance in all of Stendhal's novels, that of paternity.

Upon reflection, one can see that paternity is a dominant issue within the great tradition of the nineteenth-century novel (extending well into the

From *Reading for the Plot: Design and Intention in Narrative*. © 1984 by Peter Brooks. Vintage Books, Random House, Inc., 1984.

twentieth century), a principal embodiment of its concern with authority, legitimacy, the conflict of generations, and the transmission of wisdom. Turgenev's title, *Fathers and Sons,* sums up what is at stake in a number of the characteristic major novels of the tradition: not only *Le Rouge et le noir,* but also such novels as Balzac's *Le Père Goriot,* Mary Shelley's *Frankenstein,* Dickens's *Great Expectations,* Dostoevsky's *The Brothers Karamazov,* James's *The Princess Casamassima,* Conrad's *Lord Jim,* Gide's *Les Faux-Monnayeurs,* Joyce's *Ulysses,* Mann's *The Magic Mountain,* Faulkner's *Absalom, Absalom!,* to name only a few of the most important texts that are essentially structured by this conflict. It is characteristic of *Ulysses* as a summa of the nineteenth- and twentieth-century novel that its filial protagonist, Stephen Dedalus, should provide an overt retrospective meditation on the problem:

> Fatherhood, in the sense of conscious begetting, is unknown to man. It is a mystical estate, an apostolic succession, from only begetter to only begotten. On that mystery and not on the madonna which the cunning Italian intellect flung to the mob of Europe the church is founded and founded irremovably because founded, like the world, macro- and microcosm, upon the void. Upon incertitude, upon unlikelihood. *Amor màtris,* subjective and objective genitive, may be the only true thing in life. Paternity may be a legal fiction. Who is the father of any son that any son should love him or he any son?

Stephen's theological musing on the "apostolic succession" of fatherhood strikes to the key problem of transmission: the process by which the young protagonist of the nineteenth-century novel discovers his choices of interpretation and action in relation to a number of older figures of wisdom and authority who are rarely biological fathers—a situation that the novel often ensures by making the son an orphan, or by killing off or otherwise occulting the biological father before the text brings to maturity its dominant alternatives. The son then most often has a choice among possible fathers from whom to inherit, and in the choosing—which may entrail a succession of selections and rejections—he plays out his career of initiation into a society and into history, comes to define his own authority in the interpretation and use of social (and textual) codes.

Freud, in his well-known essay "Family Romances," develops the typical scenario based on the child's discovery that *pater semper incertus est:* the phantasy of being an adopted child whose biological parents are more exalted creatures than his actual parents, which is then superseded when the child accepts the actual mother but creates a phantasized, illegitimate father, and bastardizes siblings in favor of his own sole legitimacy. It may be significant, as Roland Barthes notes, that the child appears to "discover" the Oedipus complex and the capacity for constructing coherent narrative at about the same stage in life. The most fully developed narratives of the child become a man all seem to turn on the uncertainty of fatherhood, to use this uncertainty to unfold the romance of authority vested elsewhere, and to test the individual's claim to personal legitimacy within a struggle of different principles of authority. In the nineteenth century, these issues touch every possible register of society, history, and fiction, and nowhere more so than in France, where the continuing struggle of revolution and restoration played itself out in dramatic political upheavals and reversals throughout the century. Particularly during the Restoration, after the fall of Napoleon who seemed to incarnate the triumph of energy and youth over the resistances of age, tradition, and hierarchy, France experienced a relapse into an intense conflict of generations. France was governed by old men who had come of age during the ancien régime, Louis XVIII and Charles X (both brothers of Louis XVI), and their ministers. Titles of nobility and certificates of noncollaboration with the Napoleonic regime were necessary to recognition, and the young men of the bourgeoisie (and the people) who had seen the doors of the future open under Napoleon now found them closed. Many of the writers of the period—Stendhal, Balzac, Musset—as well as later historians converge in the diagnosis of a regime and a social structure set in resistance to the real dynamism of the country. The Revolution of 1830 appears in hindsight merely inevitable. In cultural politics, 1830 also appears as an intensely oedipal moment, best symbolized in the famous première of Victor Hugo's *Hernani,* marking the raucous victory of the young romantics and the forces of movement. And the nineteenth-century novel as a genre seems to be inseparable from the conflict of movement and resistance, revolution and restoration, and from the issues of authority and paternity, which provide not only the matter of the novel but also its structuring force, the dynamic that shapes its plot.

I want now to return from this brief sketch of the issue of paternity and authority to the plot of *Le Rouge et le noir* by way of the novel's end, by way of the guillotine that so abruptly severs Julien Sorel's life and brilliant career, and thereby threatens our efforts to construct a coherent interpretation of the novel. Just before Julien Sorel's end, the narrator tell us, "Jamais cette tête n'avait été aussi poétique qu'au moment où elle allait tomber (Never had this head been so poetic as at the moment it was about to fall)." The next moment of the text—the next sentence—it is all over, and the narrator is commenting on the style with which the head fell: "Everything took place simply, fittingly, and without any affectation on his part." In an elision typical of Stendhal, the climactic instant of decapitation is absent. We have the vibrations of the fall of the blade of the guillotine, but not the bloody moment. The elision is the more suspect in that it is not clear that Julien's head needed to fall at all. As a traditional and rationalist criticism of Stendhal used to say, Julien's shooting of Mme de Rênal—which entails his decapitation—appears arbitrary, gratuitous, insufficiently motivated. Engaged to marry the pregnant Mathilde de la Mole, adored of her as she is adored of her father, surely Julien the master plotter, the self-declared disciple of Tartuffe, could have found a way to repair the damage done to his reputation by Mme de Rênal's letter of accusation. Those other critics who try to explain Julien's act on psychological grounds merely rationalize the threat of the irrational, which is not so importantly psychological as "narratological": the scandal of the manner in which Stendhal has shattered his novel and then cut its head off. Still another scandal—and another elision—emerges in this ending because of the novel's chronology, which would place Julien's execution well into 1831. Yet in this novel subtitled "Chronicle of 1830" we have no mention of the most notable event of the year: the July Revolution. Indeed, Mme de Rênal in the last pages of the novel proposes to seek clemency for Julien by pleading with King Charles X, who had been dethroned for almost a year. The discrepancy is particularly curious in that the whole of Julien's ideology and career—of revolt, usurpation, the transgression of class lines—seems to beckon to and call for revolution. Is the guillotine that executes Julien, the "peasant in revolt" as he has called himself at his trial, a displaced figure for "les Trois Glorieuses," a revolution notable for having made no use of the guillotine? Is the catastrophic ending of Le Rouge et le noir a displaced and inverted version of the revolution that should have been?

Perhaps we have begun to sketch the outlines of a problem in narrative design and intention, in plot and its legitimating authority (including history as plot), and in the status of the end on which, traditionally, the beginning and middle depend for their retrospective meaning. We can come closer to defining the problem with two statements that Julien makes shortly before the arrival of Mme de Rênal's accusatory letter. When the Marquis de la Mole has given him a new name, M. le chevalier Julien Sorel de la Vernaye, and a commission as lieutenant in the hussars, he reflects, "After all . . . my novel is finished." Yet the novel—if not his, then whose?—will continue for another eleven chapters. Shortly after the statement just quoted, Julien receives twenty thousand francs from the marquis, with the stipulation that "M. Julien de la Vernaye"—the Sorel has now been excised—will consider this a gift from his real (that is, natural, illegitimate) father and will donate some of it to his legal father, Sorel the carpenter, who took care of him in childhood. Julien wonders if this fiction of the illegitimate aristocratic father might not be the truth after all: "Might it really be possible, he said to himself, that I am the natural son of some great noble exiled in our mountains by the terrible Napoleon? With every moment this idea seemed less improbable to him . . . My hatred for my father would be a proof . . . I would no longer be a monster!" The word "monster," as we shall see, evokes a network of references to Julien's moment of self-identification as the plebeian in revolt, the usurper, the hypocrite, the seducer, the Tartuffe, he who, in the manner of all monsters, transgresses and calls into question the normal orders of classification and regulation. But can illegitimacy rescue him from monstrosity, when throughout the novel illegitimacy has appeared the very essence of the monstrous? Can hatred for the legal father be a proof of innocence, that is, of the lack of monstrosity, of the lack of a need to act the hypocrite? If so, have we really all along been reading not a "Chronicle of 1830" but an eighteenth-century novel—by a writer such as Fielding or Marivaux—where the hero is a foundling whose aristocratic origins eventually will out, and will offer a complete retrospective motivation—and absolution—for his desire to rise in the world: usurpation recovered as natural affinity? Legitimized by illegitimacy, Julien's plot could simply be a homecoming, a *nostos,* the least transgressive, the least monstrous of narratives.

Earlier in the novel, M. de Rênal, reflecting on his children's evident preference of Julien to their father, exclaims: "Everything in this century tends to throw opprobrium on *legitimate* authority. Poor France!" The comment explicitly connects political issues of legitimacy and authority with paternity, itself inextricably bound up in the problem of legitimacy and authority. The shape and intention of the novel are tied closely to this network of issues. The way in which the novel poses the questions of authority and legitimacy might be formulated first of all in the queries: What kind of a novel is this? To what models of plot and explanation does it refer us? There occurs a striking example of this problem early in the novel (book 1, chapter 9), in the episode of the "portrait in the mattress." Julien has just learned that M. de Rênal and his servants are going to restuff the straw mattresses of the house. He turns to Mme de Rênal and begs her to "save him" by removing from his mattress, before M. de Rênal reaches it, a small cardboard box containing a portrait. And he begs her as well not to look at the portrait in the box; it is his "secret." The narrator, typically crosscutting from the perceptions of one character to those of another, tells us that Mme de Rênal's nascent love for Julien (of which she is still largely ignorant) gives her the heroic generosity of spirit necessary to perform what she takes to be an act of self-sacrifice, since she assumes that the portrait must be that of the woman Julien loves. Once she has retrieved the box and given it to Julien, she succumbs to the "horrors of jealousy." Cutting back to Julien, we find him burning the box, and we learn that it in fact contains a portrait of Napoleon—*l'usupateur,* Julien names him here—with lines of admiration scratched on its back by Julien. The misunderstanding between the two characters, where neither perceives what is at stake for the other, cannot be confined to the realm of the personal: they are living in different worlds, indeed in different novels. For Mme de Rênal, the drama has to do with love and jealousy, with amorous rivalry and the possibility of adultery. She thinks she is a character in an eighteenth-century novel of manners, *Les Egarements du coeur et de l'esprit,* perhaps, or (as one of its innocents) *Les Liaisons dangereuses.* Julien, on the contrary, is living in the world of modern narrative—post-Revolutionary, post-Napoleonic— which precisely throws into question the context of "manners" and the novel of manners, subverts its very possibility. Napoleon, the "usurper" in Julien's pertinent epithet, represents a different order of *égarement,* or wandering from the true path: the intrusion of history into society, the reversal of a stable and apparently immutable world, that of the ancien régime, which made "manners" as social and as literary code possible and necessary. If, as Julien says a few chapters later, the "fatal memory" of Napoleon will forever prevent young Frenchmen like himself from being happy, the reason is that Napoleon represented the possibility of *la carrière ouverte aux talents:* advancement through merit, the legitimation of class mobility, legalized usurpation. While Julien studies not to appear a disciple of Napoleon, he manages at various times in the novel to resemble first Robespierre, then Danton, both of whom stand behind Napoleon as destroyers of the ancien régime who, at the very least, historicized the concept of *le monde,* thus making the novel of manners in the strict definition impossible. The scene of the portrait in the mattress signals the impossibility of the novel of manners as Mme de Rênal understands it: questions of love and interpersonal relations no longer play themselves out in a closed and autonomous sphere. They are menaced by class conflict as historicized in the persistent aftermath of the French Revolution.

In a number of essays and reflections over the years, Stendhal developed an explicit theory of why the Revolution had rendered social comedy—*la comédie de Molière,* in his shorthand—impossible. He explains himself most fully in "La Comédie est impossible en 1836," where he argues that social comedy could work only with a unified audience, sharing the same code of manners and comportment, and agreeing on what was deviant and extravagant in terms of this code. The Revolution, in destroying the society of court and salon, and raising to consciousness the claims of different social classes, shattered the unity of sensibility on which Molière's effects were predicated; at a performance of *Le Bourgeois Gentilhomme* in 1836, half the audience would laugh at the would-be gentleman, Monsieur Jourdain—as was Molière's intention—but the other half would admire and approve him. When social class becomes the basis for political struggle, one man's object of ridicule becomes another man's serious social standard. The demonstration applies as well to the novel (as Stendhal noted in the margins of a copy of *Le Rouge et le noir*): the novel of manners is itself threatened with usurpation, it cannot exclude from its pages something else, something that had best be called politics. Mme de Rênal has no knowledge or understanding of politics, yet she is living in a world where all other questions, including love, eventually are held hostage to the political, and this is true as well for the novel in which she figures.

Politics in *Le Rouge et le noir* is the unassimilable other, which in fact is all too well assimilated since it determines everything: nothing can be thought in isolation from the underlying strife of legitimacy and usurpation that polarizes the system within which all other differences are inscribed and that acts as a necessary (though I refuse to say ultimate) interpretant to any message formulated in the novel. A telling illustration of this proposition occurs in chapter 18 of book 1, which describes the king's visit to Verrières and which is rich in representations of the movement from red to black, as Julien first cuts a figure in the mounted Honor Guard and then dons the cassock to assist the abbé Chélan in the magnificent *Te Deum* at the chapel of Bray-le-Haut, which so overwhelms him that in this moment "he would have fought for the Inquisition, and in good faith." It is in the midst of this religious spectacular that the narrator treacherously comments, "Such a day undoes the work of a hundred issues of Jacobin newspapers." The reader who has been paying attention will understand that this undoing has been the intent and design of the religious ceremony, staged and financed by the Marquis de la Mole: it is one more political gesture in the continuing struggle to say to whom France belongs.

But if politics is the indelible tracer dye in the social and narrative codes of the novel, the very force of the political dynamic is matched by the intensity with which it is repressed. For to admit to the force of the political is to sanction a process of change, of temporal slippage and movement forward—of history, in fact—whereas the codes of the Restoration are all overtly predicated on temporal analepsis, a recreation within history of an ahistorical past, a facsimile ancien régime that rigorously excludes the possibility of change, of revolution. Hence those who claim to be the legitimate masters of France cannot allow themselves to mention politics: the "Charter of the Drawing-Room" in the Hôtel de la Mole prohibits mockery of God and the Establishment, bans praise of Voltaire, Rousseau, and the Opposition newspapers, and decrees "especially that one never talk politics." The result is boredom, for what has been repressed is what interests everyone most passionately, and indeed ultimately motivates those acts that claim ostensibly to belong to the domain of manners, since manners themselves— such an act as changing into silk stockings and slippers for dinner—are political gestures. Politics stands as the great repressed that ever threatens to break through the bar of repression. Politics, as someone calling himself "the author" puts it in a parenthetical debate with another figure called "the publisher," is like a pistol shot in the middle of a concert. Even before Julien's pistol shot shatters the ceremony of the Mass in the church at Verrières, there is a constant threat of irruption of the political into manners, a denuding of the mechanisms governing the relations of power and of persons, an exposure of the dynamic governing history and narrative.

At stake in the play of politics and its repression is, I have suggested, the issue of legitimate authority versus usurpation; and in this opposition we find the matrix of the principal generative and governing structures of the novel. The interrelated questions of authority, legitimacy, and paternity unfold on all levels of the text: in Julien's use of models to conceive and to generate his own narrative, in the problematizing of his origins and his destiny, in the overriding question of who controls the text. To treat only briefly the first of these issues: we know that Julien from his first appearance in the novel moves in a web of bookish models, derived first of all from Las Cases's memoir of Napoleon, the *Mémorial de Sainte-Hélène,* the *Bulletins* of the Grande-Armée, and Rousseau's *Confessions,* which are then supplemented by the New Testament, which Julien has simply learned by heart, and by Joseph de Maistre's book on the papacy; to these one could add occasional references to Corneille's *Le Cid* as model of honor, and continuing citation of Molière's *Tartuffe,* another text memorized. The extent to which Julien believes in his texts of reference varies, but so does the meaning of "belief," since he has chosen to be the *hypokrites,* the player of roles. It is significant that the Abbé Pirard will note Julien's complete ignorance of Patristic doctrine: Julien's texts provide individual interpretations of models of behavior but no authoritative tradition of interpretation and conduct.

As a result, Julien continually conceives himself as the hero of his own text, and that text as something to be created, not simply endured. He creates fictions, including fictions of the self, that motivate action. The result is often inauthenticity and error, the choice of comportments dictated by models that are inappropriate. In Julien's "seduction" of Mme de Rênal, for instance, we are told that his success comes not from efforts to play the role of a consummate Don Juan but from his natural unhappiness at failing to please so beautiful a woman: when he bursts into tears, he achieves a victory his stratagems had failed to win. His sense of "duty" to "an ideal model which he proposed to imitate" indeed nearly spoils what is most attractive to Mme de Rênal, and robs Julien of the pleasure he might have experienced. Yet just when the reader is ready to judge that Julien would do better to abandon models and roles, the narrator turns around and points out that the contrived self-conceptions alone have put Julien in a position where his *naturel* can effect results. In a typically dialectical statement, the narrator tells us: "In a word, what made Julien a superior being was precisely what prevented him from enjoying the pleasure that had come his way."

Julien's fictional scenarios make him not only the actor, the feigning self, but also the stage manager of his own destiny, constantly projecting the self into the future on the basis of hypothetical plots. One of the most striking examples of such hypotheses occurs when, after receiving Mathilde's summons to come to her bedroom at one o'clock in the morning, he imagines a plot—in all senses of the term, including plot as machination, as *complot*—in which he will be seized by Mathilde's brother's valets, bound, gagged, imprisoned, and eventually poisoned. So vivid is this fiction that the narrator tells us: "Moved like a playwright by his own story, Julien was truly afraid when he entered the dining room." Such fictions may even encompass the political, as when Julien immolates his last vestiges of remorse toward the marquis—the benefactor whose daughter he is about to seduce—by evoking the fate of MM. Fontan and Magalon, political prisoners of the regime: an evocation that is factually accurate but of the most fictive relevance to his own case, as indeed, we may feel, are all his self-identifications as plebeian in revolt and peasant on the rise, since they do not correspond either to our perceptions of his identity or to his own identifications with more glorious models. Because the scenarist of self-conception cannot maintain a stable distinction between the self and its fictions, Julien must unceasingly write and rewrite the narrative of a self defined in the dialectic of its past actions and its prospective fictions.

To Julien's generation of his narrative from fictional models we can juxtapose the seriality of those figures of paternity who claim authority in his career. He is set in relationship to a series of ideal or possible fathers, but in a curious manner whereby each father figure claims authority, or has authority conferred on him, as just the moment when he is about to be replaced. The "real," or at least legal, father, Sorel the carpenter, is already well on the way to repudiation when the novel opens; his first replacement, the chirurgien-major who has bequeathed his Legion of Honor to Julien, is dead and his legacy suppressed in the movement from red to black. The paternity of the Abbé Chélan emerges in strong outline only when Julien has left him for the seminary, where the severe Abbé Pirard will eventually address Julien as *filius*. "I was hated by my father from the cradle," Julien will say to Pirard, "this was one of my greatest misfortunes; but I will no longer complain of fortune, I have found another father in you, sir." Yet this moment of overt recognition comes only in chapter 1 of Book 2, that is, after Julien's translation to Paris and his establishment in the Hôtel de la Mole: precisely the moment when Pirard begins to give way to the Marquis de la Mole, who will complicate the question of paternity and play out its various transformations.

It is at the moment of transition from Pirard's paternity to the marquis's that the question of Julien's legitimation through illegitimacy is first explicitly raised: the possibility that he might be the natural child of some aristocrat (perhaps hidden in the mountains of Franche-Comté during the Napoleonic wars), which would explain what the abbé (and later the marquis) sees as his natural nobility. For the abbé and the marquis, Julien's natural nobility is something of a scandal in the order of things, one that requires remotivation and authorization through noble blood, be it illegitimately transmitted. If, like the foundling of an eighteenth-century novel or a Moliére comedy, Julien were at last to find that he has been fathered by an aristocrat, this discovery would legitimate his exceptionality, his deviance from the normal condition of the peasant, and show that what was working as hidden design in his destiny was, as the abbé puts it, "la force du sang." The strength of bloodline would rewrite Julien's narrative as satisfactorily motivated, no longer aberrant and deviant, and rescue Julien's transgressive career, and the novel's dynamic, from the political realm by restoring them to the anodyne of manners.

A curious dialogue between the abbé and the marquis, these two believers in paternal authority and the legitimate order, explicitly formulates for the first time the theory of Julien's illegitimate nobility. The dialogue creates a chiasmus of misunderstanding concerning the anonymous gift of five hundred francs to Julien, as each speaker mistakenly infers from the other's words possession of some secret knowledge about Julien's origins and thus makes further unfounded inferences. It is through misinterpretation and the postulation of concealment—of what is "really," so far as we know, the absence of anything to be concealed—that Julien's noble illegitimacy begins to achieve textual status, to acquire an authorship based on a gratuitous play of substitutes for the origin. Further retroactive motivations for the origin then fall into line. The next step follows from Julien's duel with the Chevalier de Beauvoisis, who doesn't want it thought that he has taken the field of honor against a simple secretary to the marquis: the Chevalier hence lets it be known that Julien is the natural child of "an initimate friend of the Marquis de la Mole," and the marquis then finds it convenient to lend, as he puts it, "consistency" to this version. He will go on to furnish Julien with a blue costume in addition to the secretarial black; wearing the former, he will be the younger son of the old Duc de Chaulnes (who, I note in passing, comes to be an object of hatred to Julien, a representation of repressive authority). The marquis then authorizes the Abbé Pirard "to keep no longer the secret" of Julien's birth. The blue costume is followed by the cross (of the Legion of Honor): the cross that the legitimate son, Norbert de la Mole, has been demanding in vain for some eighteen months. This process of seemingly casual ennoblement by way of illegitimacy, motivating and promoting Julien's rise in the world through a hidden authority, will reach its climax when the recuperated and effaced plebeian makes himself—through Mathilde's pregnancy—into the natural son-in-law, himself continuing the bloodline, and stands on the verge of becoming the legal son-in-law, Mathilde's husband, the Chevalier de la Vernaye.

But I have so far said nothing about another figure of paternal authority in the narrative: the narrator. The relation of the narrator to Julien—and of all Stendhalian narrators to the young protagonists of his novels—is patently paternalistic, a mixture of censure and indulgence; the narrator sets a standard of worldly wisdom that the protagonist must repeatedly violate, yet confesses to a secret admiration for the violation, especially for *l'imprévu,* the unforeseeable, the moments when Julien breaks with the very notion of model and pattern. The narrator constantly judges Julien in relation to his chosen models, measuring his distance from them, noting his failures to understand them, his false attributions of success to them, and the fictionality of the constructions he builds from them. As Victor Brombert has so well pointed out, the Stendhalian narrator typically uses hypothetical grammatical forms, asserting that if only Julien had understood such and such, he would have done so and so, with results different from those to which he condemns himself (*Stendhal et la voie oblique*). To take just one example, which characteristically concerns what did not happen between Julien and Mme de Rênal: "If Mme de Rênal had had the slightest *sang-froid,* she would have complimented him on the reputation he had won, and Julien, with his pride set at ease, would have been gentle and amiable with her, especially since her new dress seemed to him charming." Constantly referring to the worlds of misunderstanding between his characters, the missed chances and might-have-beens, the narrator repeatedly adumbrates other novels, texts of the might-have-been-written. This obtrusive narrator, master of every consciousness in the novel, claims to demonstrate why things necessarily happened the way they did, yet inevitably he suggests the arbitrariness and contingency of every narrative turn of events, how easily it might have been otherwise.

"Paternalism" is of course a highly charged concept for Stendhal—a man who used a hundred different pseudonyms, who in his letters to his sister referred to their father as "the bastard," thereby no doubt indicating his wish to consider himself as illegitimate, and who once remarked that if you notice an old man and a young man together who have nothing to say to each other, you can be certain that they are father and son. Encoded in his novels is always the problem of whether paternity is possible, whether there might be a father and son who could talk to one another. The unfinished *Lucien Leuwen* comes closest to staging a perfect father, yet even he must eventually be rejected: as Lucien says, my father wishes my happiness, but in his own manner. It is a fault inherent to fatherhood that to act toward the son, even with the intent of aiding him in *la chasse du bonheur,* is inevitably to exercise an illegitimate (because *too* legitimate) control, to impose a model that claims authoritative (because authorial) status. All Stendhal's novels record the failure of authoritative paternity in his protagonists' lives, and at the same time demonstrate the narrator's effort to retrieve the failure by being himself the perfect father, he who can maintain the conversation with his son. Yet there comes a point in each novel where the protagonist must slip from under the control of the narrator-father as well.

Julien, it seems, slips from under the control of each of his figures of paternal authority when that control becomes too manifest. The paternal narrator seeks to restrain Julien, to circumscribe him through the deployment of the father's greater worldly wisdom, yet he also admires those moments when Julien kicks at the traces of narratorial control, creates the unforeseen. Julien's slippage from under the exercise of authority—his self-inventing, self-creating quality—typifies the highly metonymic character of the Stendhalian hero, figure of unarrested, unappeasable desire which can never be anchored in a definitive meaning, even retrospectively. The entire narrative mode of Stendhal's novels is in fact markedly metonymic, indeed virtually serial, giving the impression of a perpetual flight forward, a constant self-invention at the moment and of the moment. The Stendhalian novel appears to be a self-inventing artifact. What we know of Stendhal's habits of composition (particularly from the marginalia to the manuscript of *Lucien Leuwen*) suggests that he literally invented his fiction from day to day, using only the most meager of anecdotes as an armature. Each day's writing—or later, with *La Chartreuse de Parme,* each day's dictation—became an extrapolation of what the protagonist should become on the basis of what he had been, and done, the day before. The astonishing sense of rapidity given by these novels was matched in fact by rapidity of invention, a refusal of revision and the return backward: they are the last palimpsestic texts imaginable.

Upon reflection, one sees that Stendhal makes curiously nonretrospective use of narrative, which, I have argued, is in essence a retrospective mode, tending toward a finality that offers retrospective illumination of the whole. The Stendhalian protagonist ever looks ahead, planning the next moment, projecting the self forward through ambition: creating in front of the self, as it were, the circle of the *ambitus,* the to-be-realized. Lucien Leuwen repeatedly refers to himself as *un grand peut-être* ("a great perhaps"), and Julien, too, ever eludes fixed definitions in favor of constant becoming. The narrator generally seems concerned to judge the present moment, or at most the moment just past, rather than to delve into the buried past in search of time lost. Flaubert will epitomize the essentially retrospective nature of his own, and no doubt most, narrative when, in *L'Education sentimentale,* he has Frédéric Moreau, faced with the portraits of Diane de Poitiers at Fontainebleau, experience *concupiscence rétrospective,* desire oriented toward an irrecoverable past. Stendhal's novels, in contrast, seem to be based on *désir prospectif,* desire in and for the future. If, as Georg Lukács claims, *L'Education sentimentale* typifies the novel's organic use of time, Stendhalian time is inorganic, momentary, characterized by abruptness and discontinuity (*The Theory of the Novel*). This quality may well appear paradoxical in a novelist so preoccupied with history, which is necessarily retrospective. Yet it accords with Stendhal's political liberalism, his belief that only the future could reconcile and resolve the contradictions of the present—and, in the process, create readers capable of understanding his novels. His venture into something resembling the historical novel, in *La Chartreuse de Parme,* is indeed accomplished by making the retrospective impulse an object of satire: the powdered wigs of the court of Parma represent Restoration as make-believe, a ridiculous (and doomed) effort to set back the clocks of history. We might say that Stendhal's typical verb tense is the future perfect, that of the will-have-been-accomplished: a tense that allows for the infinite postponement of accomplishment. And this may offer one clue to the need for the arbitrary and absolute *finis* of the guillotine.

Le Rouge et le noir, in its rapid, evasive, unarrestable narrative movement, and in the narrator's games of containment and outmaneuver with the protagonist, ever tends to suggest that things might be otherwise than they are or, perhaps more accurately, that otherwise is how things are but not how they might have been. Curiously, the apparently stable figure of the triangle, which René Girard found to be the basic structure of mediated desire in the novel—where A desires B because B is desired by C—lends itself to this narrative instability and uncontrollability, since the very abstraction of the triangle figure permits a free substitution of persons at its corners (*Deceit, Desire, and the Novel*). Thus, when Julien is most profoundly unhappy at his inability to make Mathilde love him with any constancy, the novel suddenly opens up its most comic episode, the courtship of the Maréchale de Fervaques according to the formula provided, along with a volume of manuscript love letters, by the absurd Russian Prince Korasoff—an episode that is an exercise in pure, which is to say empty, style. The Russian prescribes that Julien must make love to another lady—any other lady—of Mathilde's society. Julien chooses Mme de Fervaques and manages to make eloquent speeches to her by arranging himself in the drawing room so that he appears to look at her while he is gazing past her to Mathilde, the third point of the triangle. The love letters that he daily copies and delivers are so lacking in specific pertinence to their referents that when he once forgets to make the substitution of "Paris" and "Saint-Cloud" for the "London". and "Richmond" of the original, his oversight makes no appreciable difference. Nor is their addressee of much importance: even after Mme de Fervaques has joined the dialogue and begun to answer him, he continues simply to copy Korasoff's letters. The narrator comments: "Such is the advantage of the grandiloquent style: Mme de Fervaques was not at all astonished by the lack of relationship between his replies and her letters." The grandiloquent style (*style emphatique*) stands for all that Stendhal detested in such romantic contemporaries as Chateaubriand and Victor Hugo: a grandiose inanity that was the opposite of the penetrating, denuding prose Stendhal had from childhood admired in the *philosophes* and the *idéologues*. Julien's success in bringing Mathilde to heel is assured when she opens his desk drawer and finds there a pile of Mme de Fervaques's replies in envelopes that he has not even bothered to open. What impresses her most is not simply that he should be the sentimental choice of the grand Mme de

Fervaques but that the relation should be void of content—a matter of envelopes rather than of the messages they enclose. When she falls, vanquished, at Julien's feet, her surrender is a tribute to the authority of empty style, style as pure geometry.

The emptiness generates a plenitude, for Julien's courtship of Mme de Fervaques results in Mathilde's sustained passion for Julien and in her pregnancy, a full meaning that assures the continuity that entails all Julien's future successes—title, fortune, new name. When the marquis, acting through the Abbé Pirard, suggests that Julien offer a gift "to M. Sorel, carpenter in Verrières, who took care of him in childhood," he offers overt and final realization of Julien's primordial wish not to belong to his biological father. The "family romance" has, for once, come true. The elaborate fictions of Julien's legitimation through illegitimacy may correspond to Mathilde's pregnancy from elaborate and empty games of style. The episode of Mme de Fervaques offers a remarkable demonstration of the instability of motivation in relation to result, a figure of the narrative's capacity to generate its significant structures from empty configurations, to institute new, authoritative governing structures in its apparently random flight forward. With Mathilde's pregnancy and Julien's dreams for the future of his son—he never conceives the child *in utero* as anything but a son—the past is made, retrospectively, to take on the dynastic authority that it has always lacked. By transmitting paternity and projecting it into the future, Julien can at last postulate fully the paternity that stands behind him, believe in the illegitimacy that ennobles and legitimates him. Julien by this point belongs to the Restoration, indeed stands as a figure of how restoration is carried out: by using politics to attain a place in a system of manners that then is used to efface politics, pretending that the way things came to be as they are (by revolution and reaction, for instance) does not belong to history, that the place of each thing, and person, in the structure of things is immutable.

We have worked our way back to the end, to the moment where the apparent stability achieved by Julien, his guarantee of a nonpolitical and uneventful future, is catastrophically exploded, shattered by the pistol shot in the church of Verrières, annihilated by the fall of the blade of the guillotine. We need to return here to Julien's tentative belief in his remotivated paternity—a belief expressed in a conditional of probability (translated earlier in this chapter): "Serait-il bien possible . . . que je fusse le fils naturel de quelque grand seigneur exilé dans nos montagnes par le terrible Napoléon? A chaque instant cette idée lui semblait moins improbable"—juxtaposed to its "proof" in his hatred for the legal father—"Ma haine pour mon père serait une preuve"—and the comment that with this realization of the family romance he would no longer be a monster—"Je ne serais plus un monstre"—and also his remark, a few lines earlier, that his novel is over and the merit is his alone: "Après tout, mon roman est fini, et à moi seul tout le mérite." If we can understand how hatred works to guarantee a benign origin, authorizing the political change of place and of class as necessary and nontransgressive, we still need to ask why the novel that claims to be finished continues for another eleven chapters, and why these chapters stage the return of the monster.

The word "monster" is used on a few occasions in the text. It appears to refer in particular to ingratitude, especially toward figures of paternal authority, and also to erotic transgression, usurpation, class conflict and the stance of the "plebeian in revolt," a stance that Julien tends to assume at moments of crisis (for example, upon Mathilde's declaration of love and at his trial) perhaps because it is simplifying and political, a decisive model for action. The monster figures the out-of-place, the unclassifiable, the transgressive, the desiring, the seductive. The letter that Mme de Rênal writes under the dictation of her confessor will provoke catastrophe because it sketches precisely the portrait of Julien as monster: "Poor and avid, it is by means of the most consummate hypocrisy, and by the seduction of a weak and unhappy woman, that this man has sought to make a place for himself and to become something. . . . In conscience, I am forced to think that one of his means to success in a household is to seek to seduce the most notable woman there. Covered by an appearance of distinterestedness and by phrases from novels, his sole and overriding object is to succeed in gaining control of the master of the house and his fortune." The whole letter indeed reads like an outline of *Tartuffe,* the classic story of the usurper who comes to the point of throwing the legitimate masters out of the house:

> C'est à vous d'en sortir, vous qui parlez en maître:
> La maison m'áppartient, et je le ferai connaître.
>
> (It is for you to get out, you who speak as master:
> The house belongs to me, and I shall make it known.)
> (4.7.1157–58)

This portrait of Julien has a certain truth, not only because it offers an interpretation that an unsympathetic reader might well adopt but also because it corresponds to Julien's occasional portrayals of himself as the monster. If we were looking for psychological explanations, could we not say that Julien, in attempting to kill Mme de Rênal, is seeking to kill the monster, to eradicate the person who has preserved and transmitted the monster image of himself? And perhaps he is seeking to assure as well his own eradication by assuming the monster identity—for if he dies, the monster will die with him. Such an explanation gains plausibility when we find that Julien at his trial publicly assumes this identity, calling himself a "peasant who has revolted against the lowness of his condition." In raising this political specter that everyone wants repressed, this potential of monstrous usurpation, Julien, as the abbé Frilair points out, virtually commits suicide. It is as if he were confessing to a guilt deeper than his crime in order to make sure that full punishment would ensue. And that is one way to lay the monster to rest.

But such an "explanation" seems too easy, too smooth. It covers up and reduces the scandal of the ending, and this strikes me as a mistake, especially since "ending" is a chronic scandal in Stendhal's narratives: *La Chartreuse de Parme* collapses its set so fast that three of the four major characters are done away with in the space of a few sentences, and two important novels, *Lucien Leuwen* and *Lamiel,* never managed to get finished at all. Like his admirer André Gide, Stendhal dislikes concluding. Would it, then, be more productive to think of the Stendhalian ending as a version of what the Russian Formalists called "the laying bare of the device," which here would be the very device of plotting, the need for beginning, middle, and end, which in the laying bare would be shown to be both necessary and arbitrary?

I do not want to use an appeal to what has been called in some recent criticism the *arbitraire du récit,* the gratuitous freedom of narrative, as explanatory in itself. I do, however, want to call attention to a specific and curious intrusion of the arbitrary that we find in the relation between the anecdote that served as source and armature for *Le Rouge et le noir* and the narrative discourse invented on its basis, between the "raw material" of story and its elaborations in Julien's plot. This anecdote is strangely contextualized early in the novel itself, in condensed and displaced form, as a weird indicator of things to come. I am thinking of the moment when Julien, on his way to the Rênal house for the first time, stops in the church of Verrières for a show of prayer, and finds a scrap of newspaper, on which he reads: "Details of the execution and the last moments of Louis Jenrel, executed at Besançon the. . . . " The rest of the article is torn off. Turning the scrap over he read: "The first step." That Julien also thinks he sees blood on the pavement (it is in fact water from the font, colored by light coming through the crimson curtains) adds to the sense of a foreshadowing which appears somewhat crude in the context of Stendhalian subtlety. We seem to have the intrusion within the novel of the crime, trial, and execution of Antoine Berthet: the story that Stendhal found in *La Gazette des Tribunaux,* and used as outline for his novel—a *fait-divers* covered over by the narrative discourse but only half-accommodated to its new context. That Louis Jenrel is an anagram of Julien Sorel may indicate something about the partially concealed, half-assimilated status of this anecdote in the novel: the anecdote is present in the manner of a statement displaced into a corner of a dream, demanding expansion and relocation in the process of dream interpretation. How do we read the newspaper in the novel?

The ending of the novel appears to mark a new intrusion of newspaper into novel, dictating that Julien must finish in the same manner as the prototype from whom he has so markedly deviated. That is, maybe Julien shoots Mme de Rênal and goes to the guillotine *because* that original monster Antoine Berthet shot Mme Michoud de la Tour and went to the guillotine, and here my "because" does not belong to the domain of source studies or psychological explanation but to narratology, to a perverse logic of narrative. Julien is handed over to the guillotine because the novel is collapsed back into the anecdote, the *fait-divers,* in which it originated and from which it has diverged. This outcome may on the one hand suggest that Julien's plot finally is not his own, to shape as he wills. On the other hand, it may suggest a more general suspicion of narrative invention, which appears to be subject to interference from outside texts—to the uncontrollable intrusion of a newspaper fragment, for example, that at the last constitutes a mortal intertext.

Saying that Julien attempts murder and suffers execution because he must be made to fulfill Berthet's scenario is, of course, critically perverse, but it has the advantage of not concealing the perverse relations of Stendhal's novel to Julien's. The climactic moment of *Le Rouge et le noir* may be an instance of what is known in classical rhetoric as a "metalepsis of the author": assigning to the author's agency an action that should normally have been given an agency in the text, as when one says that Vergil "makes" Dido die in book 4 of the *Aeneid,* or when Sterne or Diderot invokes the author's power to accomplish (or defer) some event in the narrative. Neither Stendhal nor the narrator so overtly appears to stagemanage events—Julien's fatal act indeed inaugurates a period of diminished narratorial intervention, as we shall see—yet the effect is similar, a denuding of the very act of narrative invention. One cannot get around the problem or the effect by claiming that Julien's narrative fills in the "details" that are torn off from the newspaper story, thus providing a new, fuller motivation for crime and execution, for it is precisely in the details pertaining to the motives for crime and execution that the text radically frustrates us. Remotivating the text here, to make it a well-behaved, docile narrative, will always require ingenious extrapolation, classically psychological in nature. It may be better to recognize that the *fait-divers* in the novel remains somewhat diverse, resisting assimilation to our usual models of seamless novelistic worlds. Although it may be perverse to read Julien's plot as motivated in its very undoing by Berthet's plot, such a reading at least forces us to face the rhetorical problem of the ending, putting before us the question of Julien's novel—in relation to Stendhal's, with its peculiar leftover, the status of which we need to determine.

We must now knit closer ties between Julien's two remarks, "My novel is finished" and "I would no longer be a monster." We have seen that "monster" alludes to the irrespressible presence of class conflict and politics, which turn on the ultimate questions: Where does legitimate authority lie? Who shall inherit France? "Monster" connotes ambition, mobility, the desire to rise and to change places, to be somewhere one doesn't belong, to become (as by seduction and usurpation) something one cannot be by definition (by birth). The monster is the figure of displacement, transgression, desire, deviance, instability, the figure of Julien's project for himself, of his projective plot. In fact, the monster is conjointly the figure of politics and of plottedness, of politics as plot and plot as politics. Plot itself—narrative design and intention—is the figure of displacement, desire leading to change of position. The plotted narrative is a deviance from or transgression of the normal, a state of abnormality and error, which alone is "narratable." What Julien identifies as his "novel" at the moment he declares it finished is precisely a deviant trajectory that has led him away from the authority of his legal origins, that has deauthorized origins and all other principles of legitimate authority, to the point where he could postulate a new authority in the theory of natural nobility. Yet, since that nobility, that legitimacy through illegitimacy, has been achieved through the deviance and usurpation of a highly political career, it is *ipso facto* tinged with monsterism. Later in the century, novels by Balzac, Hugo, Eugène Sue, Dickens, Dostoevsky, and others will exploit a world of the criminally deviant, as if the underworld of the transgressive and dangerous social elements were the last fund of "narratable" material in an increasingly bland social and literary system. Julien has no connection to the underworld, as yet undiscovered in 1830; yet his plot is already criminally deviant and transgressive, politically usurpatory. Hence what must be punished is not so much any specific act or political stance but rather the fact of having had a plot.

Can we then say that Julien Sorel is handed over to the guillotine because he has had a plot? There must be the guillotine at the end because there has been the novel, that strange excrescence of telling produced by the tissue of living. The telling perpetuates itself through more telling—scenarios for its further development, adumbrations of how it might be told otherwise—and then the simple monstrous anecdote of Antoine Berthet obtrudes again at the end, as Stendhal's reminder (to himself, to us) that to have lived in the divergence of plot, to have lived as the narratable, means somehow to be deviant, hence, in some cosmic narratological court, to be guilty. To frame Julien's novel within his own novel—to continue beyond the end of Julien's novel and take it to pieces—is Stendhal's way of having a plot and punishing it, of writing a novel and then chopping its head off.

The narrative "leftover" that follows Julien's shooting of Mme de Rênal presents a Julien already castrated of the desiring that creates the novelistic plot: no longer interested in ambition, he judges his whole Parisian experience to have been an error; no longer interested in Mathilde and his worldly marriage, he returns to the explicitly maternal embrace of Mme de Rênal. "He never thought of his successes in Paris; he was bored with them." His mode of thought and being here passes beyond the self-conceptualization and the invention of roles necessary to the plotted existence; he rejects the mediating figures essential to the creation of scenarios of desire and displacement: "One dies as one can. . . . What do *others* matter to me?" Not only does Julien appear to renounce his models in these final chapters, he seems also to move beyond the control and guidance of the paternal narrator. There is far less commentary by the narrator in these chapters; indeed his voice nearly falls silent, to leave the stage to Julien's almost uninterrupted monologue. The last four chapters following Julien's sentencing, also lack titles and epigraphs, a departure from the rest of the novel that accords with the notable effacement of the narrator's discursiveness and dramatic presence. Julien has simultaneously moved beyond paternal authority and beyond the plotted novel. He is no longer narratable material; his novel has closed shop, and the extranovelistic perspective of it closing chapters serves to underline the disjuncture between plot and life, between Julien's novel and Stendhal's, between authoritative meaning and the subversion of meaning.

It is as if Stendhal had decided to enclose within *Le Rouge et le noir* the scenario for what he liked to refer to, contemptuously, as a "novel for chambermaids." Not that Julien and his plot have much to do with chambermaids, except in his social origin, and also in the offer made to him early in the novel of Mme de Rênal's chambermaid, Elisa, as a suitable wife—an offer whose acceptance would have effectively arrested the plot of ambition, short-circuited the novel. But we may perhaps take the "chambermaid's novel" more generally as the figure of seductive literature. To read a novel—and to write one—means to be caught up in the seductive coils of a deviance: to seduce, of course, is to lead from the straight path, to create deviance and transgression. Stendhal seduces us through Julien's story, then he denounces the seduction. With the fall of the blade of the guillotine, he puts an end to the artificiality of the plotted story.

Something similar, though perhaps inverse, happens to the plotting of history in Stendhal's novel. The Revolution of 1830, as I mentioned, never manages to get represented in the novel even though in strict chronology it should; the novel as concert waits in suspense for this true historical pistol shot, which never comes. Yet the entire political dynamic of Julien's career tends toward that revolution: his personal transgression will be played out on the national theater in 1830—and then again, more savagely, in 1848 and 1871. The whole novel motivates and calls for the Revolution of 1830, as if it should be the forty-sixth chapter of book 2, the one beyond the last. In refusing to furnish us with that extra chapter, Stendhal performs a gesture similar to his dismantling of Julien's novel, suggesting that one cannot finally allow even history to write an authoritative plot for the novel.

The issue of authority, in all its manifestations, remains unresolved. Julien achieves no final relationship to any of his figures of paternity. It is indeed Sorel the carpenter who reemerges in the place of the father at the end, and Julien attributes to him the jolly thought that the expectation of a legacy of three or four hundred louis from his son will make him, like any father, happy to have that son guillotined. The fathers inherit from the sons. As for Julien's own paternity, his plan that Mme de Rênal take care of his son—whom Mathilde will neglect—goes for naught when Mme de Rênal dies three days after he does. The fate of this son—if son it be— never is known. The novel rejects not only specific fathers and authorities but the very model of authority, refusing to subscribe to paternity as an authorizing figure of novelistic relationships. Ultimately, this refusal may indicate why Stendhal has to collapse his novels as they near their endings: the figure of the narrator as father threatens domination, threatens to offer an authorized version. He too must be guillotined.

The question, who shall inherit France? is left unresolved. The question, who shall inherit from Julien Sorel? is resolved only on the financial plane; and the victory of Sorel *père* over his son is perhaps an ironic representation of the novelist's ultimate and absolute paternal power to put his creatures to death. But the novel comments further on its close and perverse relation to the guillotine when Julien, in prison, recalls Danton's grammatical musings on the eve of his death: "It's singular, the verb *to guillotine* can't be conjugated in all its tenses; one can say: 'I will be guillotined, you will be guillotined," but one doesn't say: 'I have been guillotined.' " For very good semantic reasons, the verb is grammatically defective: one cannot, in the first person, use it retrospectively. We encounter again, even here at the end, Stendhal's typical prospectivity, his predilection for the future perfect: "I will have been guillotined"—the tense of deferral, the tense that denies retrospective satisfaction. Deferral haunts as well Stendhal's relation to the "happy few" he designated as the inheritors of his message. In *La Vie de Henry Brulard,* he famously inscribes these happy few, his readers, in a future fifty or a hundred years after his time. To do so is to defer the question of readership and to temporalize the spatiality of the dialogue in which readership might be thought to consist. The uncertain reader may then, too late, want to ask of the novel why it should be thus and not otherwise: or, in the words ascribed to Beaumarchais that serve as epigraph to book 2, chapter 32: "Hélas! pourquoi ces choses et non pas d'autres?"

Le Rouge et le noir, perhaps more acutely than more "normally" plotted novels, makes us aware of both the consonances and the disjunctures of life and its telling, of event and might-have-been, of biological pattern and concerted deviance from it. Julien Sorel's brilliant, brief, transgressive, and truncated career raises in acute form questions about significant ends and their relation to generative structures of narrative. Stendhal's somewhat perverse refusal to end "naturally"—his postponement of conclusion, superseded by the catastrophic eclipse—places us before the problem of standard narrative form, the ways in which we usually understand beginnings, middles, and ends. In particular, his obsessive concern with problems of paternity and authority—on the structural and textual as well as thematic levels—makes us ask why we have fictional biographies, what we expect them to do. *Le Rouge et le noir* solicits our attention and frustrates our expectation because we have some sense of the fitting biographical pattern: one in which sons inherit from fathers and pass on, be it through Stephen Dedalus's "apostolic succession," a wisdom gained, a point of understanding attained. Stendhal's perversity may make us realize that such a patterning is both necessary and suspect, the product of an interpretation motivated by desire, and that we also must acknowledge the work of more negative forces of recurrence and revenge. How we move from beginning to end in a significant way—creating a pattern of transformation in the sequence leading from beginning to end—demands further reflection, and a more fully elaborated model for understanding, which we will find suggested in the most boldly speculative work of Freud.

Stendhal and the Uses of Reading:
Le Rouge et le noir

Ann Jefferson

Stendhal's fiction is both surrounded and inhabited by the voices of its many readers. Reading is a major preoccupation of the text, and in his "Projet d'un article sur *Le Rouge et le noir*" Stendhal defines his novel largely in terms of its readership: as a response to certain kinds of reading, and as an anticipation of others. *Le Rouge et le noir* thus becomes a dialogue with a host of other voices which serve to create polyphonic effects both as a result of this very dialogue, and through their own heterogeneity. For Stendhal's readers are of many kinds: some are desired, some despised; some are men, some are women; some are Parisian, some are provincial; some are liberal, some are not; some live on the second floor, and some on the fifth; some are contemporary, some are not yet born. But whatever the nature of the reader, the texts are written with a strong interlocutory bias, "comme une lettre à un ami," or as a substitute for conversations that can never take place, as witness the opening remarks of *Lucien Leuwen:* "Ce conte fut écrit en songeant à un petit nombre de lecteurs que je n'ai jamais vus et que je ne verrai point, ce dont bien me fâche: j'eusse trouvé tant de plaisir à passer les soirées avec eux!"

Whether or not one sees the "lecteur bénévole" so ardently invoked in *Lucien Leuwen* as one of the *happy few,* the novels are nevertheless also explicitly addressed to a much wider audience than that which comprised the Mme Rolands of 1880 or 1935. Indeed, Stendhal regards his switch from theatre to fiction as a move which enables him to accommodate a much more varied audience. In his view the democratization of theatre

From *French Studies* 37, no. 2 (April 1983). © 1983 by the Society for French Studies.

audiences since the Revolution was incompatible with the fundamentally monologic basis of comedy, and it is precisely the novel's ability to accommodate a heterogeneous audience that makes it the comedy of the nineteenth century. Comedy in the theatre is limited by the choice it has to make between the "gens grossier, incapables de comprendre les choses fines" and the "artistes qui ont l'intelligence des *scènes fines.*" It is thanks to its polyphonic structure (although Stendhal does not, of course, make his claims in these terms) that the novel has the capacity to surmount and contain these contradictions.

Indeed, in his "Projet d'un article" Stendhal specifically describes *Le Rouge* as being designed to straddle a split reading audience. This audience, he says, comprises on the one hand provincial women, and, on the other, frequenters of Parisian society. This split, based on differences in both geography and education, has, until 1830, led to the production of two quite different types of novel—"les romans pour les femmes de chambre" and "le roman des salons." "Le roman pour les femmes de chambre" is a different size from the Parisian one (in-12, as opposed to in-8°), has a different publisher (Pigoreau as opposed to Levavasseur or Gosselin), has a far bigger audience ("avant la crise commerciale de 1831, [M. Pigoreau] avait gagné un demi-million à faire pleurer les beaux yeux de province"), and has its own specific conventions as regards character and style ("le héros est toujours parfait et d'une beauté ravissante, fait *au tour* et avec de grands yeux *à fleur de tête*). The authors of these novels are M. le baron de la Mothe-Langon, M. M. Paul de Kock, Victor Ducange, etc.," they are quite unknown in Paris and their many works profoundly unsuited to Parisian tastes: "Rien ne semble plus fade, à Paris, que ce héros toujours parfait, que ces femmes malheureuses, innocentes et persécutées, des romans de femmes de chambre."

In contrast, the main aim of the Parisian author is "le mérite littéraire," and this snobbery is reflected in the expectations of his readers. Stendhal mentions Walter Scott and Manzoni as exponents of this classier genre, but they are also exceptions in that they are read as widely in the provinces as in Paris, although for quite different things:

> Les petites bourgeoises de province ne demandent à l'auteur que des scènes extraordinaires qui les mettent toutes en larmes; *peu importent les moyens* qui les amènent. Les dames de Paris au contraire, qui consomment les romans in-8°, sont sévères en diable pour les événements *extra-ordinaires.* Dès qu'un événement a l'air d'être amené à point nommé pour faire briller le héros, elles jettent le livre et l'auteur est ridicule à leurs yeux.

> C'est à cause de ces deux *exigences opposées* qu'il est si difficile
> de faire un roman qui soit lu à la fois dans la chambre des
> bourgeoises de province et dans les salons de Paris.

Stendhal sets himself the task of bridging this gap and, moreover, of doing
so in a way that will not make him the two hundred and first imitator of
Walter Scott ("Sir Walter Scott a eu environ deux cents imitateurs en
France"). He professes himself "ennuyé de tout ce moyen âge, de l'*ogive*
et de l'habillement du xvᵉ siècle," and determines to accommodate the
contradictions of his audience by treating novelistic convention with high-
handed disdain: in *Le Rouge* "il osa . . . laisser le lecteur dans une ignorance
complète sur la forme de robe que portent Mme de Rênal et Mlle de la
Mole, ses deux héroïnes, car ce roman en a deux, contre toutes les règles
suivies jusqu'ici." Imitation (of Walter Scott) can only be a temporary
solution to the problem of the "exigences opposées," as the works of the
two hundred would-be Walter Scotts survive little longer than a year or
two and are then completely forgotten. Novelistic innovation and transgression represent a more effective form of polyphony than Walter Scott's. But
it will also have to accommodate an even more heterogeneous audience—
one that includes the readers of 1880.

Unlike the contemporary provincial and Parisian audiences, this future
audience is an unknown quantity. In *Henry Brulard* Stendhal describes himself as talking to "des gens dont on ignore absolument la tournure d'esprit,
le genre d'éducation, les préjugés, la religion," and as a consequence, the
addition of this silent voice to the polyphony of the text will serve to
relativise the topicality associated with what one might call the first level
of polyphony, that is, the one that includes the provincial and the Parisian
voices of 1830. Readerly multilinguism appears thus to be associated with
two distinct projects in the novel: first, topicality in the description of the
society of 1829–30, and second, long-term survival in the hearts of the
future equivalents of Mme Roland and M. Gros. These two aims may seem
to be incompatible, but essential to both is the linking of the strategy of
multilinguism with the determination not to copy from books.

The Parisian reader plays a central role in the construction of Stendhal's
portrait of the society of 1830, and it is through him that a topical referential
reading is established. It is to a large extent by means of the appeal to the
Parisian reader's experience that the veracity of the novel's social portrait
is authenticated; for it is only the contemporary reader who can judge
whether *Le Rouge* is indeed a chronicle of 1830, and whether it lives up to
the claims for truth attributed to Danton in the novel's first epigraph. The
Parisian reader knows, like Stendhal, that France has changed beyond rec-

ognition in the first thirty years of the century, and that the image of French society and *moeurs* portrayed in the tale of Marmontel and the novels of Mme de Genlis are quite out of date ("Projet d'un article"). He is presumed, by implication, to have been a guest at "les bals de cet hiver," and more explicitly to be acquainted with the tedium of the salons: "Tout l'ennui de cette vie sans intérêt que menait Julien est dans doute partagé par le lecteur." His are the standards that are invoked by the author as guidelines for interpretation, and at the outset of the novel author and reader are clearly defined as belonging to the same Parisian world.

It is by this means that Stendhal is able to bring his two envisaged readerships into dialogue. Instead of pandering to both sets of tastes by alternating their preferences (which is how Walter Scott manages to succeed with both camps), Stendhal brings them into confrontation. The Parisian reader is set down in the provinces in the guise of the "voyageur parisien," a kind of tourist whose concerns and interpretations differ on almost every score from those of the provincials around him. He is *surprised* by M. de Rênal's nail factory, *shocked* by his air of self-satisfaction, *struck* by Sorel's sawmill—a series of small collisions which reveal the disparity in experience and presuppositions that exists between the provincial and the Parisian. Even the Parisian's view of the view, to which he turns in order to forget the asphyxiating provincial obsession with money, differs from that of the provincial; for where the Parisian reader dallies with the author "songeant aux bals de Paris abandonnés le veille," and admiring the natural beauty of the landscape, the provincial is shrewdly calculating the revenue that the tourist trade is likely to bring. These misinterpretations and surprises have to be set aright for a Parisian audience over and over again, in a manner that ends up by relativising the assumptions and conventions of both groups in question.

The Parisian needs to have provincial sayings pointed out to him ("Mme de Rênal . . . avait été la beauté du pays, *comme on dit dans ces montagnes*," my italics). He needs to be told about local practices with which he is unfamiliar—how they stuff their mattresses, for example. And his ignorance of provincial and cultural *moeurs* appears to be total: "*Rapporter du revenu* est la raison qui décide de tout dans cette petite ville qui vous semblait si jolie." He even needs Mme de Rênal herself explained to him: "Mme Rênal était une de ces femmes de province que l'on peut très bien prendre pour des sottes pendant les quinze premiers jours qu'on les voit. Elle n'avait aucune expérience de la vie, et ne se souciait pas de parler." These two factors make her incomprehensible to Parisian eyes, since experience of life and the ability to hold one's own in company are the sine qua non of Parisian success, as Julien's encounter with the salons of the Faubourg Saint-Germain illustrates. The Parisian reader is assumed to be mystified by his introduction to a character who is both exemplary and topical: in his "Projet d'un article," Stendhal claims that "cette femme [était] impossible dans les moeurs égrillardes qui envahirent la France à la mort du superbe Louis XIV en 1715 et qui ont régné jusqu'à la mort funeste de son arrière-petit-fils Louis XVI en 1793."

Through this juxtaposition of provincial and Parisian readings of the provinces Stendhal creates a dialogic effect which, as it is developed, leads to a questioning of the Parisian interpretative system that is established at the opening of the novel. The Parisian reader gradually becomes the object of a second reading. (There is, in other words, a slight shift in the diegetic status of this reader. He remains at all times, however, a characterized rather than an implied reader.) He begins to lose his interpretative authority as his values are progressively turned against him by the text, and to recede further and further from its central concerns. This process is begun in the portrait of Mme de Rênal and is continued in such characteristically ironic authorial remarks as:

> Il ne faut pas trop mal augurer de Julien; il inventait correctement les paroles d'une hypocrisie cauteleuse et prudente. Ce n'est pas mal à son âge. Quant au ton et aux gestes, il vivait avec des campagnards; il avait été privé de la vue des grands modèles. Par la suite, à peine lui eut-il été donné d'approcher de ces messieurs, qui'il fut admirable pour les gestes comme pour les paroles.

This forces the reader to endorse and acknowledge values (hypocrisy) which vanity normally makes him prefer to deny. In this case he cannot, since the remark is made with such incontrovertible aplomb by an author with whom the reader has become so inextricably identified (as a worldly Parisian).

This kind of remark continues to put the Parisian reader in an increasingly awkward position until authorial values eventually become more clearly dissociated from Parisian ones. A well known instance is the comment made about Julien's entry into the café at Besançon:

> Quelle pitié notre provincial ne va-t-il pas inspirer aux jeunes lycéens de Paris qui, à quinze ans, savent déjà entrer dans un café d'un air si distingué? Mais ces enfants, si bien stylés à quinze ans, à dix-huit tournent *au commun*.

The Parisian is invited to share his younger brother's patronizing scorn for Julien's inexperience, but is then roundly punished for having done so by being called common. On this occasion, provincial qualities are unequivocally preferred to Parisian ones.

The Parisian's role in the interpretation of the text virtually ceases to function in this explicit way beyond the end of part 1. In part 2 it is the turn of the provincial (largely in the figure of Julien) to make what he can of the Parisian world. In this reversal of roles the Parisian is still the loser, for by presenting Paris through the eyes of Julien, Stendhal creates an effect similar to that of Montesquieu's *Lettres persanes:* Parisian customs are rendered arbitrary by Julien's introduction to them. The split between Julien's view and that of the Parisian reader is made explicit at the beginning of what chapter 2 calls Julien's "Entrée dans le Monde."

> Les salons que ces messieurs [Julien and l'abbé Pirard] traversèrent au premier étage, avant d'arriver au cabinet du marquis, vous eussent semblé, ô mon lecteur, aussi tristes que magnifiques. On vous les donnerait tels qu'ils sont, que vous refuseriez de les habiter; c'est la patrie du bâillement et du raisonnement triste. Ils redoublèrent l'enchantement de Julien. Comment peut-on être malheureux, pensait-il, quand on habite un séjour aussi splendide!

Here the Parisian's experience of the world is directly relevant to the world described (Paris), unlike the provincial world of part 1. It is a world which he recognizes and understands. But as Julien gains in experience and loses his initial naivety, he seems to move further and further away from, and not closer to, this Parisian view of things. He learns to speak the "langue étrangère" of the salons, takes fencing lessons, dancing lessons, and, in short, becomes a dandy. But it is not these accomplishments that endear him to Mathilde or which make him the hero of Stendhal's novel. A split between provincial and Parisian readings thus gives way here to a split between actions and characters which are repeatedly defined as "singular" on the one hand, and Parisian interpretations of them on the other.

The word "singulier" is used to describe Julien in all the different mileiux in which he finds himself, but in Paris this singularity poses a serious threat to the Parisian reader's interpretative capacity. It is Parisians themselves who find Julien "fort singulier" in the de la Mole salon. Singularity in Stendhal is generally synonymous with a failure or an inability to comply with the reigning *convenances,* and in this case those *convenances* are the Parisian reader's main point of reference for interpretation. Mathilde too (for all that she is also baffled by Julien) shares this quality of singularity, and her exceptionality is indeed frequently alluded to in the second part of the novel. Croisenois notes that "Mathilde a de la singularité" (and adds, "c'est un inconvénient"). The author himself mentions that "ce personnage fait exception aux moeurs du siècle," although he does so in order once more to turn the novel's values against Parisian ones when he goes on: "Ce n'est pas en général le manque de prudence que l'on peut reprocher aux élèves du noble couvent du Sacré-Coeur." This crisis in reading comes to a head during Mathilde's night of *folie*.

Here the author creates further bewilderment by invoking the Parisian reader once more, only to confront his values with a character who refuses to conform to them: "Ce personnage est tout à fait d'imagination, et même imaginé bien en dehors des habitudes sociales qui parmi tous les siècles assuront un rang si distingué à la civilisation du xixᵉ siècle." The reader figure is described as one of the "âmes glacées" who are likely to take offence at this portrait, and the author goes on elaborately to dissociate them (the Parisian "âmes glacées") from the supposedly unnineteenth-century behaviour of Mathilde: "Cette page nuira de plus d'une façon au malheureux auteur. Les âmes glacées l'accuseront d'indécence. Il ne fait point l'injure aux jeunes personnes qui brillent dans les salons de Paris de supposer qu'une seule d'entre elles soit susceptible des mouvements de folie qui dégradent le caractère de Mathilde." This move seems at first to be designed to save the Parisian reader's face, but it does just the reverse, for in the next breath the author says that in fact Mathilde is part of the real world that he is portraying:

> Eh, monsieur, un roman est un miroir qui se promène sur une grande route, Tantôt il reflète à vos yeux l'azur des cieux, tantôt la fange des bourbiers de la route. Et l'homme qui porte le miroir dans sa hotte sera par vous accusé d'être immoral! Son miroir montre la fange, et vous accusez le miroir! Accusez bien plutôt le grand chemin où est le bourbier, et plus encore l'inspecteur des routes qui laisse l'eau croupir et le bourbier se former.

The Parisian's reading fails not only in its response to what lies outside his world (singularity), but, more seriously, in its response to certain aspects of his own. His touchiness on matters of decency seems to blind him to a part of the reality for which he was supposedly the key and the guarantor. Readerly *convenances* are part of a representation which they are incapable of recognizing. But without the Parisian reader to authenticate the portrait of the society of 1829–30 (a society to which he himself belongs) how is this portrait to be read?

Before answering this question, more must be said about Mathilde's topicality. Some (real) contemporary readers seem to have recognized the reality of the portait of Mathilde. Count Alexis de Saint-Priest wrote a dialogue in which one of the speakers claims to recognize the type and says: "Voulez-vous une peinture fidèle du grand monde: lisez *Rouge et noir*; faites connaissance avec mademoiselle Mathilde, le type des demoiselles du faubourg Saint-Germain. Voilà de la vérité! voilà de l'exactitude! C'est là dans toute la force du terme un auteur bien informé et un livre de bonne foi!" And Stendhal himself appears to regard the depiction of Mathilde's *amour de tête*, or *amour parisien* as a major realist achievement in his novel: "Cette peinture de l'amour parisien est absolument neuve. Il nous semble qu'on ne la trouve dans aucun livre." So that the assertion in the text that Mathilde is "imaginée bien en dehors des habitudes sociales" of the time would appear, at least in part, to be a dig at the Parisian reader's ticklishness in matters of taste. Like the pistol shot of politics she may "mortally offend" half the readership, even if she does not bore the other half. Good taste (or what the author calls *grâce*) is thus incompatible with the mirror principle, for just as the exclusion of politics from the novel would ruin the portrait of France in 1830, so too would the exclusion of Mathilde and her *amour de tête*. The harsh truths of the day (promised in the novel's first epigraph) prove to be too much for the reader of the day. There seems, in a way, to be no reader capable of recognizing the truth of Stendhal's portrait. Referentiality becomes caught in a double bind whereby the reader is asked to recognize his own world, and at the same time is shown that this world provides an inadequate framework for that recognition. The nature of the society represented prevents that representation from being fully perceived within it.

Returning now to the question of how this partially unrecognizable representation of 1830 is to be read: the novel itself contains suggestive accounts of different uses of reading which may have a bearing on the problem. There are many readers in *Le Rouge,* and reading takes many different forms. Broadly, though, reading falls into two categories: private or clandestine reading, and socially useful reading. It is this socially useful reading that characterizes the Parisian, and leads one to suspect that Stendhal's Parisian reader would not in any case be reading referentially, but strategically, as a means to further his own social advancement.

First and foremost, however, reading, according to Stendhal, is an antidote to boredom. This boredom is part of his portrait of contemporary *moeurs,* for he attributes it to social changes that have taken place since 1789 ("Projet"). Reading itself is thus an activity made necessary by the society described in the text read. It compensates for the absence of social gatherings and conversations that made life in eighteenth-century France such a pleasure, and which, according to Stendhal, still existed in the Italy of his day (witness the remarks to this effect made in *De l'amour*). Nineteenth-century French society, however, not content with simply making reading necessary, goes so far as to adapt it to its own purposes: reading is made the passport to social acceptability, even social success. There is censorship not only in what is read, but also in how it is read.

René seems to be the set text for entry into the de la Mole salon. It saves its young readers from ridicule, and provides them with the necessary model to imitate. Julien fails to read quite the right texts (despite the fact that he reads more than anyone else in the novel), and with the exception of the "volume dépareillé" of *La Nouvelle Héloïse* makes the (socially) crucial omission of fiction. Nevertheless, his initiation into society in the de la Mole household is effected by means of a testing of his reading. His time at the seminary has already taught him the social uses of reading: reading the wrong texts for the exam gets him a poor result, although his knowledge of the same texts on the occasion of this meeting with the archbishop wins him the admiration of the old man and a fine edition of Tacitus. These two events, then, prepare him for the first social hurdle encountered over the dinner table in the Faubourg Saint-Germain—a discussion of Horace. Here his response shows him in a good light for a provincial, but a poor one for a Parisian. His learning is evidently superior, but his style lamentable:

> Julien répondit en inventant ses idées, et perdit assez vite sa timidité pour montrer, non pas de l'esprit, chose impossible à qui ne sait pas la langue dont on se sert à Paris, mais il eut des idées nouvelles quoique présentées sans grâce ni à-propos et l'on vit qu'il savait parfaitement le latin.

Julien fails to conform with Parisian norms because he invents his ideas, rather than repeating the orthodoxy, and because he doesn't speak "la langue dont on se sert à Paris," a language which, to judge by other cases, is best learned parrot-fashion. Croisenois and Norbert are probably some of the best practitioners of this language—Croisenois because he is clearly such an elegant copy of René, and Norbert, because he makes no bones about wrapping up his reading in a series of "idées toutes faites." The Abbé Pirard suggests to Julien that he is likely to be asked to teach Norbert "quelques phrases toute faites, sur Cicéron et Virgile." In any case, Norbert regularly comes to the library to mug up topics for the evening's conversation: "Norbert . . . venait étudier un journal, pour pouvoir parler politique le soir." Society seems, then, to determine the form that reading should take and the uses to which it should be put: imitation and repetition. Under these circumstances, *Le Rouge et le noir* itself seems particularly unsuitable for a Parisian reading. It constantly offends standards of decent amusement (e.g., Mathilde's night of "folie"), renders its culminating action inimitable, and, as the next part of the argument will show, invites another kind of reading which more or less precludes any repeatable "phrase toute faite."

The second form of reading that the text represents is clandestine reading, which is offered as an alternative to social reading. Mathilde and Julien are the main secretive readers in the text. Their self-imposed secrecy is partly the result of censorship, for both read politically unacceptable texts: Julien reads Napoleon at night in the Rênal household, his lamp hidden in an upturned vase, and Mathilde, whose clandestine reading is mainly political, comes by her texts through theft. She steals books from the library, and indeed theft itself seems to become a main motive for reading in her case. For example, the private collection of "nouveautés un peu piquantes" which Julien is responsible for buying on the marquis's behalf, is regularly purloined: "[Julien] eut bientôt la certitude que pour peu que ces livres nouveaux fussent hostiles aux intérêts du trône et de l'autel, ils ne tardaient pas à disparaître. Certes ce n'était pas Norbert qui lisait." Nevertheless, neither Mathilde's nor Julien's motives are genuinely political; for both of them, reading offers models which happen to be socially unacceptable: Napoleon for Julien, Marguerite de Navarre for Mathilde. This type of reading is subversive to the extent that its texts are censored, its heroes unorthodox and its mode clandestine. But it shares with Parisian habits the aim of imitation, and thus belongs ultimately to that camp.

The alternatives to the impossible referential reading of *Le Rouge* are not limited to these socially more or less acceptable repetitions and imitations. A rather different experience of reading is indicated by Saint-Giraud in the mail-coach that takes Julien to Paris: "un bon livre est un événement pour moi," he says on his brief appearance which, in many ways, constitutes one of the novel's densest moments of reflexivity. This "performative" mode of reading contrasts significantly with the socially utilitarian and imitative readings which are far more frequently evoked in the novel. And if this performative mode does indeed represent a serious and viable alternative, the question of referentiality may, for the time being, be suspended.

In *Henry Brulard* reading is represented almost exclusively as event. It is very similar to Mathilde's sixteenth-century ideal of love: "il n'était pas l'amusement de la vie, il la changeait." Brulard's reading is a series of decisive events which leave a permanent effect on his life and personality. The discovery of *Don Quixote* was "peut-être la plus grande époque de [s]a vie"; Aristo "forma [s]on caractère"; and without Horace and Euripides he would have succumbed to the tyranny of Raillane and become "un excellent jésuite . . . ou un soldat crapuleux, coureur de filles et de cabarets." The intervention of books in his life is of unsurpassed importance for two reasons: first, because these books become the grid through which he constructs and interprets his experience (this factor is, of course, not without its dangers); and second, because the reading of them constitutes a kind of experience which is matched by very few other things.

Le Rouge itself does not offer its ("real") reader any model of a performative reading to follow, not least perhaps because to do so would be to introduce imitation into this reading process and so undermine its essential status as event. Instead it elicits such a reading through its repeated use of the *imprévu* and through comedy. *Rêverie* and *hilarité,* the two main reader responses that these strategies instigate, are the two inseparable experiential forms that a performative reading of *Le Rouge* would take.

As the novel moves towards its finish, the incidence of what it calls *folie* and *l'imprévu* significantly increases. The shooting episode as a whole is *imprévu,* and is composed of largely inexplicable elements. In the Castex edition the notes to chapter 35 (the shooting) and 36 (Julien's imprisonment) consist mainly of explanations to fill out the elliptical utterances of the narrative. For instance, the brusque "Adieu" with which Julien parts from Mathilde is felt to require expansion and clarification. So is the following sentence: "Julien sauta à bas du fiacre, et courut à sa chaise de poste," where the lack of clear motive needs, apparently, to be compensated for. The reason why Julien is unable to form the words of a letter to Mathilde gives rise to further editorial intervention and a discussion of divergent scholarly responses: according to Martineau, Julien is in the grip of "un tremblement nerveux qui l'empêche d'écrire," whereas Castex suggests that the problem may be due to the poor suspension of the post-chaise in which Julien is travelling. In either case it is clear that this is an instance of what Wolfgang Iser would call a blank or a gap that needs to be filled by the reader. The number of blanks at this point is extremely high, and the question is: what sort of procedure should be used to fill them?

On this the text is not nearly so directive as Iser's model would suggest, and the reader is confronted with a thoroughgoing indeterminacy concerning the appropriate level of reading. Castex, in accordance with the principles of good scholarship, has gone for a purely referential reading of the particular blank under discussion: stagecoaches of 1830 offered a far smoother ride than the faster post-chaises. Martineau's reading at this point is based on the conventions of psychological realism associated with a certain kind of fiction. It assumes that the hero's feelings and emotional responses are the main object of the text. Neither reading, however, explains why the blank should be there in the first place, and, in a sense, the alacrity with which they rush to fill the gap gives them a certain resemblance to Mme de la Mole and the other *grandes dames* who are so offended by Julien's unconventional behaviour on his arrival in the salon: "L'imprévu produit par la sensibilité [in this case Julien's] est l'horreur des grandes dames; c'est l'antipode des convenances." The *imprévu* of Julien's actions at the climax of the novel is, precisely, a flouting of reading *convenances,* be they scholarly, psychological or what.

Even Stendhal himself seems to have bridled somewhat at the degree of *imprévu* in his text—at least on the level of style. He complains of it in *Henry Brulard*, and it is a recurrent theme in his notes in the Civita Vecchia copy of the text: the style, he says, is "trop abrupt, trop heurte," and he recommends to himself, "Ajouter des mots . . . pour aider l'imagination à se figurer." But it does seem that it is the impoverished imagination of the *âmes glacées* that he has in mind, and there are two marginalia in chapter 17 of part 1 which would support this view: "Pas assez développé. Qu'est–ce que cette bataille? diront *les gens sans esprit;*" and "Quelle rapidité! Pour *les demi-sots,* n'est-ce pas de la sécheresse?" (my italics). The *âmes sensibles* can presumably cope with the *imprévu* and the reason for this may well be their mode of reading, which is not dependent on *convenances*. Certainly no convention-bound reading can deal with the increase of *folie* that occurs towards the end of the novel. As Shoshana Felman remarks, *folie* tends to appear with gathering frequency towards the end of each of the novels, and *Le Rouge et le noir* is no exception. And, as she also points out, the mark of the *fou* is his lack of a common language with others (including, in this instance, the reader), and his inability to make his "parole solitaire" understood. *Folie* and its cognate *singularité* are terms which are associated first with Mathilde, and then, more extensively, with Julien; this characteristic indicates that the conventional assumptions which form the basis of most readings may not be adequate to their task in this last part of the novel.

If the *âmes sensibles* succeed in making sense of the final pages of the novel, this is because their reading is not grounded in any particular kind of language, or any particular set of conventions. Their reading must necessarily be conducted in a state of hilarity and revery, and they will be profoundly moved by it. In Stendhal's world, these three things (hilarity, revery, and *attendrissement*) tend to go together, and laughter is an essential prerequisite for being moved. In *Henry Brulard* he claims that his love of *opera buffa* is due to the fact that only in this genre can he be moved to tears: "Je ne puis ètre touché jusqu'à l'attendrissement *qu' après un passage comique*" (Stendhal's italics).

There are many kinds of laughter in Stendhal, but this particular and vital form depends on a freedom from both convention and referentiality. Of all Stendhal's heroes, Lucien Leuwen is probably the most prone to laughter, and this tendency can probably be correlated with the particuarly hide-bound nature of the society in which he moves. Nancy is obsessed with *convenances,* and Lucien's first outburst of laughter is provoked by his encounter with the utterly proper and utterly self-important prefect, M. Fléron. The effect of the man's appearance is enough to produce an uncontrollable explosion of laughter in Lucien, which is echoed time and again in the novel. *Le Rouge* represents an equally sober world where laughter is proscribed by the *convenances.* It is explicitly forbidden in the de la Mole salon where "il n'était convenable de plaisanter de rien." But precisely because of the hold of these rules, there is statistically more laughter in this part of the novel than in any of the others. Julien himself has two notable moments of this *rire fou*: once in Verrières (in a chapter significantly entitled "Façons d'agir en 1830") after his Jesuitical conversation with Maugiron, the sub-prefect ("A peine M. de Maugiron sorti, Julien se mit à rire comme un fou"); and once in Paris when Mme de Fervaques enquires about the references to London and Richmond in Julien's latest letter to her. No one is more hide-bound than she, nothing more conventional than the letters that Julien writes to her, so that his response is inevitably to "céder au rire fou." The element of *folie* in these outbursts is what makes them genuine moments of hilarity, and not instances of *le rire affecté* which is the social conformist's response to all that he regards as "ridicule."

The only other moment of this sort of hilarity occurs on the visit of the singer Geronimo to the Rênal household. As a singer and an Italian, he is the antithesis of all that provincial France stands for. The exaggeratedly foreign accent in which he tells his comic tale has the children in fits of laughter, and the comic aria he sings reduces everyone to tears through laughing. The prime feature of this laughter is its essential gaiety, its total lack of malice and self-interest. The effectiveness of laughter as an antidote to *convenances* lies in this gaiety and the element of *folie* that it implies. It is the laughter of the *opera buffa* and the only possible prelude to *attendrissement.*

Stendhal devotes a number of pages to comedy and its attendant *rire fou* in his essay *Racine et Shakespeare.* Borrowing from Hobbes he defines laughter as "cette convulsion physique . . . produite par la vue imprévue de notre supériorité sur autrui," and he lays considerable stress on the element of *imprévu* in this process. The *imprévu* takes comedy out of any context of convention or conformity which preclude genuine laughter. Falstaff is the epitome of the *rire fou* because of his capacity for gaiety. Molière, in contrast, is associated with a false laughter, *le rire affecté,* which is based on revenge. His comedy is therefore essentially not comedy at all, but satire, a product of the society in which he wrote and which was obsessed with the imitation of a certain model. Imitation and reference are incompatible with *le rire gai.* Laughter is a reprieve from the obligaton to imitate: "si j'entre au théâtre, je veux qu'on me fasse rire, et je ne songe à imiter personne." Equally, hilarity has to be dissociated from the referential mode of satire which is always directed at targets in social reality. If the *happy few* who read *Lucien Leuwen* are to participate in Lucien's outbursts of laughter, it must be at the expense to contemporary France:

> Cette chose si amusante, la satire personnelle, ne convient donc point, par malheur, à la narration d'une histoire. Le lecteur est tout occupé à comparer mon portrait à l'original grotesque, ou même odieux, de lui bien connu.

In other words, both modes associated with a Parisian reading of Stendhal (referential and imitative) are unequivocally excluded from the hilarious performative reading that is elicited from the *happy few*. That hilarity is an appropriate response to *Le Rouge* can be inferred from a prophetic remark that Stendhal makes a *Racine et Shakespeare:*

> Enfin, si l'on veut me faire rire malgré le sérieux profond que me donnent la bourse et la politique, et les haines des partis, il faut que des gens passionnés se trompent, sous me yeux, d'une manière plaisante, sur le chemin qui les mène au bonheur.

This would seem to describe exactly the story of *Le Rouge et le noir.*

The novel should, therefore, be seen as a Stendhalian kind of *opera buffa,* in which any hilarity provoked would be accompanied by *attendrissement.* It certainly alternates moments of comedy with moments of more emotive appeal, and perhaps nowhere more strikingly so than in its representations of love. Each affair is initiated by an irresistibly comic *quid pro quo* as each partner misinterprets the motives of the other. And yet, at the same time, love is clearly a matter to be taken seriously and properly responded to. As the first of the "Projets de préface" to *De l'amour* makes clear, reading about love depends on the reader's experience of love: "Il faut, pour suivre avec intérèt un *examen philosophique* [or, in the case of *Le Rouge,* a novelistic portrayal] de ce sentiment, autre chose que de l'esprit chez le lecteur; it est de toute nécessité qu'il ait vu l'amour." The reading of a text is, in Stendhal's view, only possible if the experiences that it represents are reevoked and recreated *within* the reader. They cannot simply remain on the page.

This emphasis on experiential reduplication gives the question of referentiality a rather different twist. Representational accuracy in the text itself has no necessary link with readerly experience which is the only basis for guaranteeing the truth of the text. According to Stendhal, no representation can ever be fully realistic because it is never taken or mistaken for reality. If we admire a landscape by Claude Lorrain, "ce n'est pas que nous supposions les arbres que nous voyons capables de nous donner de l'ombre, ou que nous songions à puiser de l'eau à ces fontaines si limpides." The effect of the painting depends rather on the pleasure it elicits, in which case, "nous nous *figurons vivement* le plaisir que nous aurions à nous promener auprès de ces fraîches fontaines et à l'ombre de ces beaux arbres." The illusion of reality is not in the text but in the reader, and it is the product of the text's power to move him or her (since Mme Roland is, so to speak, the incarnation of the *âme sensible* or the happy reader in question, the introduction of the feminine pronoun is timely). An *âme glacée* will remain unaffected by the most poignant depictions of love and persist in seeing in them only folly. The painters of the *beau idéal,* as Stendhal calls them (Raphael and Correggio) are in themselves neither more nor less realistic in this sense than the *peintres miroirs,* such as Guaspre, Poussin and the Dutch school. In both cases,

> On se sent tout à plongé dans une rêverie profonde, comme à la vue des bois et de *leur vaste silence.* On songe avec profondeur à ses plus chères illusions; on les trouve moins improbables; bientôt on en jouit comme de réalités. On parle à ce qu'on aime, on ose l'interroger, on écoute ses réponses.

Performative readings become the only relevant index of lifelikeness however improbable or *invraisemblable* the issues in question.

It is therefore the readers whom Stendhal never met, those who were ten or twelve years old when he wrote *Souvenirs d'égotisme,* those of 1880, those of 1935, perhaps even those of 1980, who have the best chance of achieving such a reading. They are less likely to be seduced by the irrelevance of referentiality, and are assumed to be less bound by *convenances,* less likely to be in search of a model to imitate. In *Henry Brulard* Stendhal is delighted at the thought of writing for this unknown audience. "Parler à des gens dont on ignore absolument la tournure d'esprit, le genre d'éducation, les préjugés, la religion! Quel encouragement à être *vrai,* et simplement *vrai,* il n'y a que cela qui tienne." When the performative reading becomes the only possible reading, only then can the text's truthfulness be properly assessed. Stendhal gains the place he hoped for alongside the "immortal *Tom Jones"* by resisting the temptation to conform to the *convenances* of his day, and by not writing like the Jesuit that he could so easily otherwise have become.

This performative reading has a dual standing within the text. At one level it forms part of the polyphony of reading which the novel activates, a voice among many other voices. But at a second level, it is the only reading that can itself accommodate the disjunctions and contradictions of that polyphony. Through it Stendhal manages to resolve and reassess the problems of representation in fiction: being set up as an alternative to a simple referential mode, it serves to relativize that mode, and to question the basis on which it functions (the vanity of the Parisian reader). As both an element of, and a recipient of, the whole polyphonic spectrum of readings in *Le Rouge et le noir* it has the effect of also relativizing that spectrum, and so bringing them to consciousness as object discourses that can be perceived as such. Finally, by placing the criterion of realism in the reader and not in the text, it raises the question of what kind of writing is required of realist fiction if, as Stendhal writes in the *Vie de Henry Brulard,*

> Un roman est comme un archet, la caisse du violon *qui rend les sons* c'est l'âme du lecteur.

Generic Survival: *Le Rouge et le noir* and the Epistolary Tradition

Margaret Mauldon

When a new narrative mode evolves and replaces an earlier convention, the new mode does not necessarily totally reject the form it supplants but may preserve some of its features. Those narrative features surviving from a prior tradition do not however retain their original meaning, but are transformed by the dynamics of their new setting. This continuing process of narrative regeneration through absorption and displacement can be discerned in Stendhal's *Le Rouge et le noir,* which contains traces of the epistolary convention, a mode highly favoured, of course, during the preceding century. But the epistolary instances of *Le Rouge* are located in a text dominated by an intrusive narrator and characterized by frequent shifts in narrative perspective and distance. They acquire from their contextual isolation overtones of irony and parody, and serve purposes which differ profoundly from those of the epistolary norm.

By the time *Le Rouge et le noir* was published (1830) the letter novel was no longer in vogue but had not entirely disappeared. Balzac's epistolary *Mémoires de deux jeunes mariées,* for example, dates from a decade later. Stendhal did not, however, need to look to contemporary fiction for epistolary models, as we know from his *Vie de Henry Brulard;* his youthful consumption of novels such as *Les Liaisons dangereuses* and *La Nouvelle Héloïse* sufficiently explains his evident familiarity with the genre. It can easily be demonstrated that in *Le Rouge* Stendhal draws on the epistolary tradition in various ways. The first rendezvous between Julien and Mathilde

From *French Studies* 38, no. 4 (October 1984). © 1984 by the Society for French Studies.

is arranged by letter; later, Julien's epistolary courtship of the devout Mme de Fervaques revives Mathilde's love by making her jealous. It is a letter which destroys Julien's hopes of marrying Mathilde and precipitates his attempt on the life of Mme de Rênal. Letters are clearly an important source of action, up to the point where Julien abandons Paris and his ambitions and returns to Verrières in search of his own true destiny.

There is of course nothing particularly surprising about the fact that the characters in the novel engage in correspondence. Letters were vital to the functioning of society in the early nineteenth century, indeed Julien's skills as a letter writer constitute an essential element in his worldly success, since he gains access to the Hôtel de le Mole because the marquis needs a reliable secretary. It is striking, however, that where epistolary exchange is actually represented in *Le Rouge* it serves not as a means of strengthening confidential personal relationships but instead as a means of manipulation and deception. Obviously, Stendhal was influenced by Laclos; there are numerous instances in *Le Rouge* of letters which mislead, or threaten, or deceive, or betray. Furthermore, letters are shown to be essentially vulnerable. The theme of censorship and of the imprudence of using letters for communication appears in many guises in *Le Rouge* and emerges most dramatically in the episode of the *note secrète* (book 2, chap. 21). It is because of Julien's remarkable memory that the effete aristocrats must use him— an outsider—to convey their vital message abroad, since they dare not entrust it to writing. Several crucial incidents of the plot are based on the assumption that correspondence is open to abuse. Letters are intercepted and never received by the addressee, or are read by someone other than the addressee, or are composed by someone other than the apparent *épistolier*. In the seminary, Julien never receives Mme de Rênal's letters, but these are perused most attentively by the Abbé Pirard. Pirard himself, on reading the request for support for Julien from his old friend the Abbé Chélan, remarks on this letter's brevity, adding: "par le temps qui court, on ne saurait écrire trop peu." So dangerous is the written word that Pirard and Julien agree on a nonverbal sign—a leaf inserted into a seemingly impersonal communication—as the safest way to inform Julien that he should leave the seminary and come to Paris. One might indeed claim that Stendhal has written an antiepistolary novel, happily relinquishing the traditional possibilities of the letter as narrative *vehicle,* and exploiting instead at the level of plot the themes of epistolary vulnerability and manipulation exemplified by the model of *Les Liaisons dangereuses.*

Stendhal, then, not only retains from the epistolary tradition the use of the letter as instigator of action, he also incorporates into the thematic level of his narrative the topic of written communication, using it to focus satirical commentary on contemporary society. While neither one of these enterprises appears particularly new, a close reading of some of the epistolary incidents in *Le Rouge* reveals that they have other more interesting functions. At one level Stendhal parodies epistolary narrative technique in complex and subtle ways, and at a more profound level he uses epistolary incidents to examine the adequacy of language as a basis for interpersonal communication.

The first significant epistolary event in the novel concerns the anonymous letter sent to M. de Rênal by Valenod, informing him of the affair between Mme de Rênal and Julien. Unable to speak freely to Julien, Mme de Rênal writes to him. Her letter is a curious document, for it is both a passionate incoherent love letter and, at the same time, a carefully calculated set of insturctions for the charade she and Julien are about to enact. Furthermore, embedded in Mme de Rênal's letter is a quite separate epistolary text, namely the model for the "anonymous" message Julien is to provide. Mme de Rênal's opening paragraphs contain familiar echoes of the traditional feminine love-letter: reproaches, self-abasement and joy that the very act of writing should place her in Julien's power: "Ne m'aimes-tu pas? es-tu las de mes folies, de mes remords, impie? Veux-tu me perdre? Je t'en donne un moyen facile. Va, montre cette lettre dans tout Verrières. . . ." The passionate tone accords perfectly with the description of the letter as hastily written, ill-spelt and tear-stained. Equally predictable, in terms of the convention, is the reckless style of delivery: the letter is sent via a servant, inside a book whose cover bears the message *"Guardate alla pagina 130."* Yet it is this same rash communication which proposes, in minute detail, an ingenious plan for averting the danger which threatens the lovers. Mme de Rênal instructs Julien in exactly how to produce the message she has composed: he is to "write" it using words and letters cut out of a printed book. The spurious anonymous letter therefore has a multiple fictional status; it is, one may say, "made up," being physically composed of fictional material, and also of course essentially fictional, since it is intended to convey an illusion. But at the same time, however ingeniously deceptive it may be in its imitation of Valenod's "façons de parler," what it implies is true, since Julien and Mme de Rênal are indeed lovers.

Mme de Rênal's intention is to redirect her husband's jealousy on to Valenod, who had in the past attempted to woo her and whose letters she still possesses. She believes M. de Rênal will consider it normal that she should have kept Valenod's letters, and that he will be desperate to find them. M. de Rênal in fact behaves exactly according to the epistolary stereotype of the jealous husband, frantically breaking open his wife's writing desk and coffers and prising up pieces of parquet in his frenzied search. Just as Mme de Rênal intends, M. de Rênal compares the letters he finds with those his wife and he have received, and concludes from the similarity of writing paper and phraseology that their origin is the same. Seen from the perspective of the epistolary canon, Mme de Rênal's plan succeeds because of the power of the tradition on which it draws. She uses a commonplace of epistolary narrative—the preservation and discovery of love letters—as a means of out-maneuvering her husband. M. de Rênal is caught in a trap of literary origin. But that is not all. Mme de Rênal's letter to Julien belongs simultaneously to two different epistolary categories, namely, the letter of love and the letter of intrigue. In epistolary fiction these categories are normally discrete, so that the juxtaposition in one message of expressions of passion with details of a cool-headed plot is unexpected. In brief, two incompatible styles of letter are conjoined, and by this conjunction undermine one another, creating comic dissonances ("[A]rme-toi de patience et d'une paire de ciseaux"). The problem of how to read Mme de Rênal's letter is compounded by the presence of the Valenod imitation, which offers an implied commentary on the text which frames it. Already intentionally derivative at the level of style, the anonymous message will physically consist of a patchwork of words cut out from a printed source. It therefore reminds the reader how difficult it is to write authentically, in language free from echoes of another's voice, and from traces of words already circulating in literary works.

The above incident thus embodies an instance of fusion between the representation of an event in the story, and the evocation of an outmoded literary vehicle which the present narrative has rejected as a means of expression. I now move forward to the early stages of the love affair between Julien and Mathilde, where once again references to the epistolary code focus attention on the contamination of literary language and the limitations of interpersonal communication. In chapters 8 to 13 of book 2 Mathilde's admiration for her father's secretary develops into what she believe is love, while Julien's increasing interest in her is equalled by his profound suspicion of her intentions. It is Mathilde who declares herself first. This bold acceptance of sexual initiative by a woman is rendered credible by the careful details we are given of Mathilde's character and reading habits, and by the atmosphere of rigid constraint which informs every aspect of conduct in the Hôtel de la Mole. Nor do we find it surprising that Mathilde should elect to write, rather than speak. Epistolary fiction has provided her with an abundance of models, and she is an avid reader. The text of her letter is not given; it is simply described as a declaration of love. After receiving Julien's cautious reply, however, Mathilde does not stop writing; indeed she writes three letters within twenty-four hours, and two of these she hands over in person. Mathilde clearly prefers writing to speaking, a fact later comically confirmed by her acute embarrassment when she has to speak to Julien after inviting him into her bedroom. She tells herself on that occasion: "Il faut cependant que je lui parle . . . , cela est dans les convenances, on parle à son amant." The narrative deliberately foregrounds the literary precedents which inspire the behaviour of Mathilde and Julien throughout this sequence. On receiving Mathilde's second letter Julien observes that he is involved in an epistolary novel: "Il paraît que ceci va être le roman par lettres," and on receiving her third, he concludes that the whole affair must be a dangerous practical joke engineered by Mathilde and her vapid friends for the purpose of obtaining compromising *written* responses. Much of the comedy of this sequence derives from the fact that the two protagonists model their behaviour on incompatible literary traditions: initially, Mathilde draws on sentimental epistolary sources, whereas Julien's reactions to her initiative derive rather from the adventure story. He imagines himself set upon by servants, robbed of Mathilde's letters, cast into a cellar and there poisoned, and so forth.

Mathilde's feeling for Julien is literary in origin: "Elle repassa dans sa tête toutes les descriptions de passion qu'elle avait lues dans *Manon Lescaut, La Nouvelle Héloïse, Les Lettres d'une religieuse portugaise*, etc., etc." Significantly, two of these are epistolary novels. Fiction confirms her hopes: she is indeed in love, and in love with someone whose social unacceptability accords with the heroic role she has adopted as her own. Julien is not the first man to whom Mathilde has written. It is by exploiting and infringing epistolary conventions in both the literary and the social sense that Mathilde has attempted on past occasions to enliven her monotonous existence and test the mettle of her suitors. When the Marquis de Croisenois attempted to gain her favour by returning to her an indiscreet letter, we are told that she ignored him for six weeks. Nevertheless, the decision to write *first*, as she does to Julien, is a bold step of which she is consciously proud: "Elle écrivait *la première* (quel mot terrible!) à un homme placé dans les derniers rangs de la société. . . . Et encore parler était affreux, mais écrire!" It is evident that the very act of writing it heightens for Mathilde the significance of her declaration of love. In her behaviour, it is impossible to distinguish rebellion against social dictates from identification with literary models: but such confusion itself parallels in a curious fashion a fundamental characteristic of the letter novel. By the claims of authenticity, of nonfictional

status, which it traditionally asserts, epistolary narrative relies on the merg-
ing in the mind of the reader of literary and "real life" criteria. The appeal
of the epistolary form depends partly on the fact that the letter is a literary
vehicle with which all readers are personally familiar, in which they themselves can record or read about daily events and emotions, thus transforming
life into narrative. For Mathilde, then, the letter offers a bridge between
real life and fiction: she attempts to draw herself into her own narrative.

It is interesting to consider these epistolary events not simply as a
nonspecific parody of the love affair by letter, but in terms of a specific
model: *La Nouvelle Héloïse*. The similarities are readily apparent: the social
inequality of the lovers, their pedagogical relationship—Julien guides Mathilde's reading as Saint-Preux does Julie's—the nocturnal tryst, the pregnancy and so forth. In both novels, the prospect of separation motivates
the first exchange of letters. Saint-Preux's initial declaration is associated
with threats of departure and hints of suicide. Julie then responds. In similar
fashion, Julien's imminent departure on a business trip prompts Mathilde
to write: "Votre départ m'oblige à parler." Later Julien regrets his decision
not to leave, arguing that absence would have nourished Mathilde's passion,
an idea powerfully confirmed by the epistolary canon. In particular, Saint-
Preux's absence on his travels in the Valais precipitates Julie's fall; when he
returns, they become lovers.

Julien knows *La Nouvelle Héloïse* so well that he quotes from it during
the crucial bedroom scene in order to fill in the embarrassing silences. But
although Rousseau's novel constitutes an undeniable intertext in this part
of the narrative, it is clearly not a model which has been faithfully imitated.
Rousseau's formula is there but its terms have been reversed. It can surely
be no coincidence that Julien's name should itself suggest, by its reference
to his celebrated epistolary forbear, the total transformation which the
canonical model has undergone. (In this context we might remember that
Stendhal entitled an early version of his novel *Julien,* thereby stressing the
connection with Rousseau's *Julie, ou La Nouvelle Héloïse.*) Three initial love
letters begging for an unambiguous response exist in both novels, but in
Le Rouge it is the woman, not the man, who makes the opening declaration,
and it is the man, not the woman, who appears hesitant and virginal. The
comic details of Julien's elaborate precautions in copying Mathilde's letters
and ensuring the safety of the originals parody an important theme of
epistolary fiction, which portrays a love letter as a potentially dangerous
possession that must be kept hidden from prying eyes. This security is
traditionally provided by that familiar figure of the epistolary world, the
confidant. So Julien duly conceals Mathilde's compromising first letter in

the cover of a large bible which he sends to his childhood friend Fouqué. But here again, it is the man rather than the woman who appears obsessed by the need for prudence and discretion. Why, one may ask, should Stendhal choose this particular sequence to parody the epistolary convention and one of its most famous exemplars? I suggest that the epistolary preliminaries to the affair between Julien and Mathilde offer a gloss on the nature of their relationship. Initially, the couple communicate by imitating an outmoded literary medium whose narrative *raison d'être* depends on keeping protagonists apart. In the first actual meeting of the lovers in Mathilde's room, the inauthenticity of their relationship becomes cruelly apparent; unable even to speak to each other comfortably, they find lovemaking a disappointment. Life and literature do not coincide.

Occasionally, parodic strategies will be deployed at the expense of purely technical aspects of epistolary narrative. For example, the style of Julien's response to Mathilde's first letter comically exposes the difficulties epistolary authors encounter in conveying essential narrative information to the outside reader. In real life, friends or lovers who correspond usually share a common background and do not need to tell each other certain things. But in fiction, this background material must often be spelled out for the benefit of the outside reader, whose needs take precedence over those of the postulated narratee. In the case of single-voiced letter novels, significant material from the missing side of the correspondence must also sometimes be included for the sake of clarity. On such occasions, the insertion into the reply of abundant quotations from the letter received provides an easy if inelegant solution. Julien's reply to Mathilde highlights both these technical narrative problems and consequently reads like a parody of a bad epistolary exposition:

> "Quoi! mademoiselle . . . , c'est Mlle de La Mole qui, par les mains d'Arsène, laquais de son père, fait remettre une lettre trop séduisante à un pauvre charpentier du Jura, sans doute pour se jouer de sa simplicité. . . ." Et il transcrivait les phrases les plus claires de la lettre qu'il venait de recevoir.

By fusing together passages from Mathilde's letter with his own, Julien believes he will render the document useless as a weapon to be used against him. He in fact adopts a clumsy authorial strategy, intended to bridge gaps in communication between author and reader, as a tactic for embarrassing Mathilde. This incident, like that of the anonymous letter, illustrates the way Stendhal uses representation of a narrative event to probe the inadequacies of a favoured fictional mode.

After Mathilde breaks off their relationship Julien resorts to devious epistolary tactics in order to regain her love. He painstakingly copies out and delivers to Mme de Fervaques's home the fifty-three model letters provided by his mentor prince Korasoff, following the prescribed programme of courtship with tenacious exactitude. The satire of the epistolary code is here overt, since the precise instructions regarding the manner of delivering the letters, their timing and length, and the careful gradation of their contents are all guaranteed to be efficacious regardless of circumstances. In fact, so totally unrelated to reality are these letters that when Julien forgets to alter the details of place names in the originals—which were addressed to an English quakeress—no harm is done. Julien does not bother to open, let alone read, the replies he receives from Mme de Fervaques. Mathilde's resistance breaks down when she discovers a pile of these unopened letters in Julien's bureau drawer. This episode reduces to the level of absurdity the notion of epistolary courtship. The letters sent by Julien are devoid of real content; they have meaning only as tokens of exchange in an accepted social ritual. But here again Julien uses an epistolary manoeuvre for his own purposes. The writing of these interminable letters does indeed convey a message, but it is a message directed at Mathilde. The traditional concept of seduction by letter is turned inside out in this narrative sequence, its only meaning that of an empty ritualized gesture, its true purpose the seduction of a lady who is never addressed.

In conclusion I should like to widen the focus of my remarks and consider the function of epistolary incidents within the economy of the entire narrative. One way of reading *Le Rouge et le noir* is to see it as a contrapuntal exploration of the differing levels of insincerity which characterize communcation both *between* individuals and also *within* the mind of a single individual. As Julien learns to recognize and to exploit the varied ways in which the world presents itself to his consciousness, not only does he learn how to use society, he learns also, though without realizing it, that society can never give him what he desires. When, during his last days in prison, Julien is isolated from the world, he discovers that nothing matters except the love he and Mme de Rênal share.

I would suggest that there is a connection between the final lesson Julien learns and the fact that, in recording his hero's accession to this truth, Stendhal parodies the epistolary form. The epistolary mode is essentially a social mode of expression. It seemingly offers, at least to the naive reader, the illusion that language is transparent and can be used for unmediated communication. But it is not surprising that *Les Liaisons dangereuses* should be the last of the great epistolary works. Laclos's novel demonstrates with relentless logic the way language can always function as a tool of persuasion and deception, both of the "other" and of the self. It exploits to the limit the potential of epistolary narrative, and contains the seeds of its decay. Stendhal learned the lesson Laclos had taught. It is no accident that in *Le Rouge et le noir* he should so entertainingly expose the conceptual flaws and technical ineptitudes of a narrative mode which had originally proposed a deceptively optimistic view of the nature of language. *Le Rouge et le noir* is in fact a catalogue of miscommunications: of misleading roles assumed or imposed, of mistaken identities, of misunderstandings, misrepresentations, and misreadings.

What's in a Name:
Ur-texts, *Hors-texte,* Intertexts

Carol A. Mossman

THE EDGES OF TEXT

"On m'appelle Julien," timidly ventures the hero when coaxed into speech by Mme de Rênal. There is something disingenuous about the wavering proferral of this name, for, at one level, the name of the son, "Julien," dictates the narrative destiny of *Le Rouge et le noir.* Amid all the strategies to eradicate the patronym (the overbearing name-of-the-father), not the least important goal is to retrieve the son's name from its eclipse.

Building on Starobinsky's equation of patricide and the erasure of the father's name, I propose that the laying bare of the filionym furthers the work of Oedipal iconoclasm which is being operated on virtually all registers of the text. Once the son's name is fully denuded, several proto-narratives will suggest themselves. Some of these interlock to form Julien's plot. Others contribute to the story which frames the novel of ambition. And through this commingling *Le Rouge et le noir* emerges as a palimpsest whose manifest plot harbors only faint recollections of any originary narratives. Here again, one of the classical Freudian assumptions—that of the existence of a latent discourse—is being translated to the forum of narratology. However, with this difference: it is no longer a matter of the individual words obtruding from beyond, but rather of whole story lines which have been, in a manner of speaking, repressed.

The notion of edge can again be invoked to good purpose in this discussion. As we have already seen, Julien's novel has elapsed between the

105

poised edge of the sawmill blade and the sharpened edge of the guillotine. These blades, in their turn, define the edges of the subsumed text which is performed, like a play within a play, inside the boundaries of a larger signifying structure. In fact, frames and edges are mutually implicating: if one conceives the text in terms of frames, the perspective becomes a totalizing one; if in terms of edges, the part is valorized over the whole. And the entire intertextual problematics which bases itself on the discourse of the *other* text—where it begins and where it ends—can be formulated as a question of frames.

The now celebrated newspaper articles which subtend *Le Rouge et le noir* had early been hailed as sources of the novel. Both of these *faits divers* were published in the *Gazette des Tribunaux* between 1827 and 1829; the reports recounted similar tales of seduction, crime and punishment. In 1846 the author's cousin and life-long friend, Romain Colomb, made the connection between *Le Rouge* and the Berthet case. Stendhal himself mentions the Lafargue crime in *Promenades dans Rome*, as Faguet pointed out for the first time.

Le Rouge's plot has often been ascribed to (and "explained" by) these mini-texts. Speculation has had it that the sources were amplified, with the plot straying somewhat from its originals, at length to be collapsed back onto the already published ending, a beheading death. Actually, it is only Julien's story which refers back to these reports. Regardless of the extent to which the novel draws its inspiration from lived experience, ultimately *Le Rouge et le noir* remains circumscribed by the literary discourse; in the end, fictional structures will take over where the real has left off.

It is as if the novel felt obliged to designate its sources—in a reminder however oblique—by incorporating those generative newspaper articles. As Julien wanders into the Verrières church he is filled with forebodings of a terrible fate. And the entire edifice is transformed into an incarnadine space.

The hero then chances on a torn piece of paper which bears his own name in anagrammatic form and predicts (at the same time as it retells) the story of Julien's execution: "Détails de l'exécution . . . de Louis Jenrel, exécuté à Besançon, le . . . ," it reads. This obtrusion of journalism into the novel presents a *fait accompli* which remains to be accomplished. The execution is at once the novel's past and its future, just as the primal father dictates fate from beyond the grave. With "Louis Jenrel," for the first time in the text one remarks the Stendhalian penchant for obscuring names, hinting that the name in its very utterance demands to be decoded and reduced to a different referent. Julien's name is camouflaged here, but so maladroitly that it cannot fail to be recognized. For slower readers, Stendhal has been accommodating. Sighs Julien: "Pauvre malheureux . . . son nom finit comme le mien." The "outre-tombe" sensation surrounding this prediction will be reinforced by each intertext, which tells a tale, only for it to be retold in the course of the novel.

One more remark should be made regarding the augury of the beginning: in spite of its suggestiveness, the details of the death are withheld. The description of Julien Sorel's death at the end runs as follows: "Tout se passa simplement, convenablement, et de sa part sans aucune affectation." The ellipsis of the beginning is thus preserved at the moment when the prophecy is fulfilled. Like the silence in which Conrad enshrouds Lord Jim's sole ignoble act, that rupture towards which the novel of blades is tending occurs in the space of a textual blackout. This novelistic "temps mort" also obscures the moment at which the fictional register intervenes and overtakes the "factual."

Now, taken as the ending to the novel of blades, the beheading can be construed as an act of castration. Such painful "operations," as we have already seen, must be covert ones. Nevertheless, it is in justifying a similar ellipsis, that of Julien's sojourn in the seminary, that Stendhal reveals the wherefores of description withheld:

> Ce n'est pas que [des faits clairs et précis sur cette époque de la vie de Julien] nous manquent, bien au contraire; mais, peut-être ce qu'il vit au Séminaire est'il trop noir pour le coloris modéré que l'on a cherché. . . . Les contemporains qui souffrent de certaines choses ne peuvent s'en souvenir qu'avec une *horreur* qui *paralyse* tout autre plaisir, même celui de lire un conte (my emphasis).

The moderate shades which the narrator ostentatiously chooses, however, are already darkened by the likes of "horror." Such terms can pertain only to a limited set of crimes, namely, those set aside by society as taboo. Mere mention of the horror-inspiring memory (a once-and-future-event) constitutes an act debilitating—castrating—in itself. Nonetheless, just as the narrator obliges us with the wherefores of the final severance's repression in displaced form, the event itself in its bloody materiality is articulated by retrojecting it onto the beginning of the novel in the Verrières cycle. There the reader, still uninitiated into the narrative scheme, does encounter a bleeding neck and, moreover, one which seems to bleed perpetually. The member in question here is the neck of the martyr St. Clement, to whose "relic" the King of ★★★ pays homage early in the novel. Its stream, frankly

gushing in Verrières, will become diverted in Besançon and thereafter reduced to a trickle in the discourse of *Le Rouge.* Figured in the itinerary of
martyrs from Clement (Verrières) to St. John (Besançon) and ultimately to
St. Julien is the itinerary of repression.

The Novel's Incorporation of Other Texts

From the onset and the choice of the *faits divers,* then, the textual
enclosure has been breached by an Ur-text, just one of several *hors-texte*
which will be brought to bear on the content and design of *Le Rouge.* With
the insertion of the journalistic intertext, which is placed in the church in
order to be read, one stands forewarned that the textual borders can be
transgressed. However, instead of *basing* himself on the celebrated newspaper article, it is as if Stendhal were attempting to invert the origination
process, so that the newspaper article would report the events recounted
in the novel. This inversion operates as follows: when, at last, Mathilde
grants Julien a nocturnal rendezvous, he is wary. Following still another
premonition of death, he decides to send an account of his life, including
the La Mole story in its unfinished version, to his convenient postal-box
friend, Fouqué. Only in the event of Julien's death is Fouqué to read this
"conte," and in such a case he is instructed to change the names and submit
the "récit" to several newspapers. Later, after events have taken a turn for
the worse, Julien frets: "Malheureusement, mon nom paraîtra dans les
journaux"—as well it does.

Just as Julien was temporarily able to reconstitute his genealogy, it
would seem that the novel reconstructs its own relation of fact to fiction
according to the following emended sequence: the testament which was
formulated as a defensive act in Paris reached Fouqué, who then commu-
nicated it to the newspapers. It was, of course, completed by the tragic
events which subsequently became public knowledge. The name of Julien
Sorel was changed to, say, Antoine Berthet with the same stroke that
converted fiction into truth. Thus, the process of inversion (and subversion)
of origins, previously examined in the context of the family, touches on
textual creation itself.

At another point in *Le Rouge,* the process of creation through decon-
struction of another text is almost teasingly staged. Valenod sends his political rival, Rênal, a letter denouncing the liaison in which his wife is
indulging with their young tutor. In an effort to parry this accusation (acting
in the belief that two wrongs can make a right), Mme de Rênal conceives
the ingenious plan of "writing" another letter of denunciation and "hon-

estly" showing this letter to her husband with a convincing display of indignation.

Julien is assigned the task of constructing this letter materially, since Mme de Rênal has herself already formulated its contents. Equipped with a pair of scissors, he snips up and destroys another text, reconstituting one of his own with the dismembered words. A few strokes of the scissors, and the reader is once again witness to the composition of a fiction whose creation depends on a genuinely inspired text. The counterfeit then accedes to the same status of authenticity as the original letter, at least in the eyes of M. de Rênal, who accepts it as an original. Origins begin to lose their referential anchors, authenticity proves unfathomable, and the Word plays a subversive role in this comedy of falsification.

Julien's enterprise of creating a text out of someone else's is distinctly reminiscent of the author's own appropriation of exterior sources for the composition of his novel. Not only, it would seem, has Stendhal apportioned himself a *fait divers,* whence to compose a piece of literature, thence to defictionalize it, but he has also captured himself in the act, like an artist who includes himself painting the court portrait.

One might even say that young Sorel is in the business of using other people's texts. It will be remembered that he woos the religious prude, Mme de Fervaques, by exploiting a readymade body of letters. Scribe that he is, Julien simply recopies this second-hand romance, observing its own plot sequence. When this correspondence seems to be culminating in a happy ending, and Mme de Fervaques is becoming more indulgent towards him, Julien drops it: because the conclusion he has all along been seeking relates to a different narrative, the story of Mathilde's seduction. Once again, incomplete and fraudulent use of one plot furthers another, and the quest for a frame leaves edges exposed.

As just noted, the collapse and incorporation of the epistolary text exercises its narrative efficacity in a different arena: Mathilde finally capitulates. From this point, Julien rapidly gravitates to the top of the world, where lo! the reader learns that he or she has been reading more than one novel: "Après tout," declares the hero fully 75 pages prior to the end, "mon roman est fini. . . . " Like the découpage episode and the epistolary exchange, Julien's novel reveals itself to be a text which is entrenched in another fictional structure. Perhaps in ignorance, the reader has been bemusedly eyeing these cameo texts, little suspecting that Julien's story might be circumscribed by another, just as the reader could hardly have realized that "la petite ville de Verrières" has stood in the shadows of Besançon and Paris. To invoke Plato's allegory of the cave (which, in fact, bears a certain kinship to Freud's vision, ever dimming through repetition, of the father), the novel constantly seems to point to a text somewhere in the distance beyond. More than midway through the novel, the reader is confronted with the disorienting possibility of novels within a novel and endings beyond the end.

Part of *Le Rouge et le noir*'s narrative scaffolding consists of an outside text which has become internalized to create a sort of inner novel, the so-called "roman de Julien." Ostensibly, textual origins become inverted, as was shown in the case of Julien's instructions to Fouqué regarding posthumous publication of the Sorel story. This kind of involution, besides confounding the clarity of beginnings, can be said to be paradigmatic of that originary movement which triggers repetition—the primary repression which sets the machine into motion.

A different sort of textual transgression occurs when, in the course of the narrative, but unbeknownst to the reader, Julien has written a story in praise of the Old Surgeon, or, otherwise stated, a history of his personal origins. This tale written within the confines of the text proper refers back to a past not depicted in the novel and elsewhere only alluded to. That is, the Old Surgeon tale reaches into the past beyond all textual borders and incorporates this past into Julien's novel, but only as a signifier of origins. *Le Rouge* refuses the reader any knowledge of its contents, which, moreover, in no way inform subsequent narrative action. As an incorporated, but stubbornly unrevealed story, it remains on the level of a pure signifier denoting an extratextual past, one buried, then partially exhumed, proffered, and then refused. It stands as an allusion to the impenetrability of origins.

THE FAMILY ROMANCE OF MATHILDE DE LA MOLE

So much for the texts which purport to be texts. Their participation in *Le Rouge et le noir* can be characterized only as subversive of clear narrative demarcation and, ultimately, of origins. Let us now turn to those texts which are not allegedly such. While these do not impinge upon the novel's pages in any material way, they nonetheless determine the novel's organization and are, like the Surgeon and Napoleon, the more present for remaining undesignated.

Repeated mention has been made of the partial narrative scaffolding furnished by the Berthet and Lafargue *faits divers*. What these outline are the hero's rise and fall. What they exclude are tales of origins and the curious aftermath of the beheading; in short, they compose Julien's novel. There is another text explicitly present in the novel—part of a family saga—which intertwines with the *faits divers* in a sort of narratological coupling to yield the complete novel, at least in the form of its manifest plot. This other text, absent at the beginning, imposes itself gradually, until it includes and then supersedes its journalistic mate. Henceforth it will be referred to as "Mathilde's novel."

Her novel makes its first official appearance in the Paris cycle, although, as we shall learn, it has been present since the beginning and even tacitly in Julien's name. Significantly, the initial revelation of her novel takes the form of a tale which seeks to explain how Mathilde has come to wear the black of mourning once a year. It is the uninspired academician, another of those creatures of the La Mole establishment, who tells Julien the story of the illustrious La Mole forebear. Briefly, it goes like this: several centuries ago, Boniface de la Mole had been cropped by a headlength as punishment for political insurgency. His mistress, Marguerite de Navarre, in a perverted gesture of heroism, then asked for his head—*plat unique*—which she buried at midnight. This deed Mathilde annually commemorates (indeed, fetishizes) by donning black, thereby identifying herself with the courageous Marguerite of yesteryear. (Mathilde is further linked through her middle name, Marguerite, a premonition that access to alternate narratives can be gained through the name.)

The narrative threads seem to be converging over the hapless head of Julien Sorel. The beginning of the novel, with Julien's near fall under the sawmill blade, his father's bullying and the somewhat ominous episode of the church, has scarcely boded well; now, with a heroine who seems bent on playing out her own past (just as, for that matter, Julien has been playing out Berthet's), the outcome for him is hardly promising.

Disregarding (but not excluding) the logic of character explanations, Julien's choice of death can already be considered to be a fate which is overdetermined narratologically. For not only is he submitting to a destiny dictated by the newspaper reports, thus deferring to the extratextual, but he is also figuring in Mathilde's romance and submitting to her will to repetition. The two narratives, Julien's and Mathilde's, are mutually compatible in that both demand the beheading death of Julien Sorel, though one continues the story beyond this point. Thus, from the strictly narratological viewpoint, *Le Rouge et le noir* interweaves stories in such a way that the decapitation becomes inevitable. And, while none of the tales in itself suffices to yield the outcome, which includes Julien's burial (that is, the red plus the black), their juncture defies alternative.

If Julien's novel seeks to turn on its origins and instate itself in their place (*fait divers*↔novel), the same holds true for Mathilde's. Boniface de La Mole's plot—the narrative of a bygone usurpation punished by castration—is a retrospective event which becomes Mathilde's adoptive text. The saga is repatriated into the novel's bosom, thereafter to be restaged—repeated—and ultimately reconstituted into a present event. Once again, we see at play the drama of a violent past, rememorated, commemorated and appropriated for a future fulfillment.

Few names command the evocative richness of "Julien." Its mere utterance suggests the names of several emperors of classical antiquity, a whole papal lineage and saints historic as well as folkloric. Indeed, *Julien* had been this novel's originally proposed title, one which, according to Romain Colomb, was not changed to *Le Rouge et le noir* until 1830, when it had already reached its publisher, Levavasseur. In spite of this last-minute change (construable, again, as an obscuring of source), Stendhal persisted in identifying his novel as *Julien* in subsequent allusions to it.

In the 1820s there was a figure from the annals of Roman history who attracted considerable public notice for the parallels which were felt to exist between that period of time (4th century A.D.) and the France of the First Empire and Restoration. This was the emperor Flavius Claudius Julianus, recognized by the Church as Julian the Apostate.

Now, Stendahl, who was known to his contemporaries as a writer of "Lives," was well versed in the biographies of the Roman artists, popes, saints and emperors, as any reader of his *Promenades* will readily perceive. And twice he attempted to write a biography of Napoleon, once at the beginning of his career (1817–18) and again towards its end (1836–37). The figure of the heroic Napoleon never ceased to haunt him.

But it is when one notices the remarkable similarities which obtain between the biographies of these two emperors that one begins to become aware of the complexity of the Stendhalian literary enterprise. Many scholars have maintained that Stendhal was lacking in invention: if such was the case, then it is more than likely that his free appropriations of others' texts and their *superimposition* were a compensatory activity. To refer again to the *Promenades dans Rome* (composed immediately prior to *Le Rouge*), it is clear that Stendhal conceives that city as a grid, with history recorded spatially rather than sequentially. For Stendhal (in company with Du Bellay and Butor), the story of Roman antiquity topographically subtends the story of the Church of Rome, and his discussions of the seven hills take the form of historical excavations with emphasis on the place where time stops and historical periods become coextensive.

On the manifest level, Julien's and Mathilde's novels overlap, interlock together to define the narrative in its full length. But Julien's story looks to Berthet, Lafargue and even Napoleon, while Mathilde's harks back to the tale of her celebrated counterpart, Marguerite de Navarre. Nor does the layering stop here. The son's name designates another filial narrative, that of Julian the Apostate, which—in this continuous line of retrospective pointing to—implicates the final figure of our intertextual itinerary. And, in spite of the complexity of this grid of corresponding narratives, the stories underlying Mathilde's and Julien's, no matter what their depth, retain their discreteness at the same time as their relation to each other as text framed and framing.

Flavius Claudius Julianus can strike one as two different men, depending on whether one relies on historical accounts of his life or on certain ecclesiastical interpretations. I will here read his biography along both lines: the first reading will aim at a comparison with Napoleon, while the second will make use of the connections drawn by popular hagiographer Jacques de Voragine in his *Légende dorée* (the *Legenda aurea*).

This Roman Julian was one of the last proponents of neo-Platonism. Beholding in the surgent Christian religion an intolerant and persecutionary force, the emperor persisted in championing a nearly obsolete Hellenic humanism (recalling the respective nostalgias of Napoleon for Rome and Julien Sorel for Napoleon).

An heir to the Roman throne and consequently a target for elimination, Julianus had spent his youth in concealment at a monastery, where he made professions of great religious zeal. Later, he was called back from his studies to aid in subduing the Gauls. Riding a tide of military victories, Julianus attained to such popularity that, on his brother's death, his own soldiers proclaimed him emperor of Rome. (Again, Napoleon is not far off.)

He thence proceeded to free Paris from the ravages of the Allemani tribes; he restored order to that city, rebuilt it and endeared himself to the populace by promulgating tax reforms (evoking the massive reforms enacted in the wake of the French Revolution). Ever expanding his empire, Julianus led his military forces over the globe in a conquest of Constantinople and Persia (here one thinks of the Napoleonic conquest of Egypt), where he was at last killed in battle.

Let us now turn to a different rendition of this same life. Julian the Apostate figures prominently in Voragine's listing of the various St. Julians—not that he ever approached sainthood, but ostensibly his notoriety was such as to merit him inclusion in this hagiographic document. The contempt in which this emperor was held by the Church is best expressed by Voragine himself:

> Il y eut encore un autre Julien, celui-ci ne fut pas un saint, mais
> un grand scélérat. C'est Julien l'apostat. Il fut d'abord moine et
> il affectait de grands sentiments de religion. . . . Il avait été in-
> struit dès son enfance dans l'art magique et cette science lui
> convenait fort.

Voragine elaborates on Julian's character in a subsequent entry devoted to
St. John and St. Paul: "Julien, craignant d'eprouver de la part de Constance
le même sort que son frère [death], entra dans un monastère, où en *affectant*
une grande dévotion, il fut ordonné *lecteur*" (my emphasis). He tells John
the Apostle:

> J'ai été élevé à la cléricature, et si je l'avais voulu, je serais parvenu
> au premier rang de l'Eglise, mais considérant que c'était chose
> vaine de vivre dans la paresse et l'oisiveté, j'ai préféré l'état
> militaire, et j'ai sacrifié aux dieux dont la protection m'a élevé
> à l'empire.

It is difficult to overlook the fact that the hypocrisies of Julianus and
Julien take the same form. Moreover, fusing the two accounts of the Apostate's life results in a personality harboring the same paradoxes as young
Sorel's: a man who conceals his contempt of religion behind its very habit,
a man of action and conquests whose disdain for the principles of Chris-
tianity only serves to valorize a certain nobility of ideals. Doubtless in *Le
Rouge* the battlegrounds have been resituated and pared down. Nonetheless,
Julien pursues his goals with military resolution, looking to Napoleon for
inspiration as Napoleon gazed at Rome and the way Rome, in the person
of that other Julian, contemplated Athens. Thebes is not far off.

By now one might wonder what else is in a name. And the question
would be well put, since intertextuality does pose a problem of limits. Julian
the Apostate is associated with two different St. Johns, one the Evangelist
and the other the Baptist, both of whose decapitated heads, according to
some accounts, finished their itineraries in Gaul. According to Voragine,
Julian the Apostate was responsible for the death of the apostle John when
the latter refused to repudiate his Christian faith.

Now, Julianus is also officially held responsible for the so-called "second martyrdom" of St. John the Baptist, the first of which had occurred
some four centuries earlier at his actual death. As religious accounts would
have it, many miracles were taking place in the vicinity of the Forerunner's
tomb, much to the consternation of the Apostate. In order to put a halt to
this phenomenon, Julianus ordered the saintly bones exhumed and scattered,

whence he was further dismayed to find that he had merely increased the radius of the miracles. So he had the bones burned, although some escaped (and multiplied) to find their way to thousands of reliquaries in the world. Reports Voragine: "C'est, en quelque sorte, un second martyre que saint Jean souffre, puisqu'il est brûlé dans ses os, et c'est la raison pour laquelle l'Eglise célèbre cette fête comme si elle était son second martyre."

THE TALES OF JOHN THE BAPTIST

If the subject of St. John has been brought up, it is because he is one of the two martyred saints mentioned in *Le Rouge et le noir,* both of whom are associated with those singular moments of timelessness and exaltation which Julien Sorel enjoys on two occasions in the novel—both times in church.

Although John's mention occurs without epithet, his identity as the Baptist rather than the Apostle becomes evident during the Corpus Christi ritual in Besançon, which liturgically requires the presence of the Baptist in his capacity as precursor of Christ. The saint makes his textual appearance during that episode in the Besançon cycle in which Julien distinguishes himself by successfully climbing a ladder to decorate and glorify the church. It is while he is teetering in these ecclesiastical heights that Julien Sorel becomes infused with a rather eroticized sense of euphoria which in fact climaxes with his perception of so many youths dressed as St. John: "L'odeur de l'encens et des feuilles de roses jetées devant le saint-sacrement, par les petits enfants déguisés en saint Jean, acheva de l'exalter." (It should not be forgotten that the presence of children in *Le Rouge* infallibly evokes a Julien Sorel *enfant* who is then, in this passage, identified with St. John through a transitive association: John→children→Julien.)

While no reference is made here to the Baptist's fate, martyrdom through beheading had been earlier signified under similar circumstances. In this other instance of ceremonial-inspired euphoria which took place in the church at Bray-le-Haut, the statue of St. Clement's perpetually bleeding neck—a reminder of his decapitation—had twice been mentioned in a strikingly short space of text: "Il avait au cou une large blessure d'où le sang semblait couler. L'artiste s'était surpassé; ses yeux mourants, mais pleins de grâce, étaient à demi fermés. Une moustache naissante ornait cette bouche. . . ." Two paragraphs later, from the mouth of the Bishop of Agde: "Ces serviteurs faibles, persécutés, assassinés sur la terre, comme vous le voyez par la blessure *encore sanglante* de saint Clément, ils triomphent au ciel" (my emphasis).

Rarely in *Le Rouge,* as has already been remarked, is description of even the most rudimentary sort found; we know little of Julien's physical aspect, nothing whatever of Mme de Rênal, and with Mathilde the reader is treated to a descriptive excess: she is blond with pale blue eyes. Thus, in relative terms Clement's statue receives over-ample treatment, sufficient to set it apart. Indeed, the salient point is the wound in his neck, still bleeding. What strikes one is how this neck can so textually pour forth, whereas Julien Sorel's will shed nary a public drop. The ellipsis of Julien's decapitation—this textual hiatus—has been displaced safely onto the beginning, a secure distance from its true referent. Nonetheless, from the beginning of the narrative the wound bleeds continuously, although increasingly covertly as the end draws nigh.

It is in the cycle following this initial grisly preview in Verrières that St. John is mentioned. And, although both his strict identity as the Baptist and his mode of death have been excised from the text consistent with a movement of accumulating repression, the effect remains as strong: the same ambiance of exaltation reigns here as in the Bray-le-Haut episode. What is being signaled in these churches, albeit with decreasing audibility, is the fate of decapitation. Julien is identified with these saints through his fate, as well as obliquely through his Christian name. (In fact, in another such displacement onto the beginning the reader encounters the name "Saint Jean," here the Rênals' domestic.)

Following the thread in this onomastic labyrinth that links Julian the Apostate to St. John the Baptist, we are at last led to one of the major intertextual configurations underlying *Le Rouge et le noir.* Voragine has effected the step into the deeper past with this neat equation: "De même qu'Hérode qui fit couper la tête à saint Jean, subit le châtiment de ses crimes, de même aussi, Julien l'Apostat, qui fit brûler ses os, fut frappé par la vengeance divine.

While the circumstances surrounding the death of St. John the Baptist are well-known to us, it might surprise the reader to learn that the original scriptural records of it have little to offer. Its official New Testament reporting is found in Matthew and Mark. Both are scant in information and, moreover, at variance with each other. According to the testimony of Matthew, Salome (she is not mentioned by name) had been prompted by her mother to ask for the head of John, and it was with regret that Herod granted her request because, although he resented the forerunner, he also feared the rebellious force of the multitude who backed the ascete.

Mark's version is more sketetal still: he makes no mention of the mother Herodias's influence over her daughter in demanding the head, nor is Herod's fear of the rabble evoked. In fact, here Herold does genuinely regret putting the holy man to death because it is said that he enjoyed hearing him orate. It is interesting that the beheading death of John is both times presented as a flashback inserted into Christ's narrative: hearing of this other worker of miracles, Jesus of Nazareth, the apparently guilt-racked Tetrarch is certain that John has returned from the dead. And so it is that John, a son figure sometimes depicted as a fomenter of rebellion, is associated with Christ in birth as in death.

There are endless variants of this legend, most of which accumulated during the fourth and fifth centuries and are recorded in the writings of Jerome and Augustine. These legends were later subject to considerble embellishment during the Middle Ages: Voragine's accounts stand out as examples of such narratological touching up. Moreover, as Kermode has demonstrated in his *Genesis of Secrecy,* there is every likelihood that the St. John episode had been superimposed on previous Old Testament legends which recounted similar events. The existence of such intertexts would point to a narrative substratum, in much the way that *La Rouge* suggests apocryphal texts. In any event, a substantial halo of folklore has collected about the head of St. John, as much in artistic circles as in the literary sphere.

Like Napoleon and Julien Sorel, John the Baptist is inalterably a son figure. First, as is frequently the case with characters destined to be considered filial, the circumstances of his birth are ascribed a peculiar importance: to an aged and hitherto sterile couple, Zacharias and his wife Elizabeth, an angel predicted the birth of a son. Zacharias, voicing doubts on the matter, was forthwith struck dumb for the duration of his son's gestation. When the Virgin Mary came to care for her aging pregnant cousin, John stirred in his mother's womb in recogintion of Mary's sacred unborn burden. Upon John's birth his father's tongue was unfettered, presumably to sing the Lord's praises. It is as if the son, John, had usurped his gift of prophecy and affinity for the Word (for he was a powerful orator) from his own father's tongue-bound condition while he was himself *in utero. . . .* In any case, he is another in the long line of filial figures already treated who politically endangers the father's (here, Herod's) hegemony by seemingly inciting to conspiracy.

For our purposes, it is the skeletal structure of the events surrounding John's beheading which bears such close resemblance to that part of *Le Rouge et le noir* which is Mathilde's novel, but in which Julien's fate is implicated as well. There can be no doubt that Julien's story tends towards the beheading death of its hero. What signals its identification with the John the Baptist legend is partially this decollation itself, but especially its curious aftermath.

The events surrounding both deaths form a single constellation: Mme de Rênal denounces Julien in a letter which is the prime cause of Julien's imprisonment/Herodias demands the death of John; Julien denounces the paternalistic society of the nineteenth century/John denounces the general corruption of his time and prescribes purificatory baptisms; Julien is judged to be guilty by his male peers for reasons ostensibly political/Herod is fearful of the Baptist because of his potent political following and does permit—by some accounts, encourages—the beheading death; Julien's severed remains are carried to his friend Fouqué/the head of John the Baptist is presented on a silver platter to Salome, who then gives it to her mother.

MATHILDE'S ROMANCE AND SALOME

Now, what follows on Julien Sorel's decapitation is a figure which is anticipatory of latter-day conceptions of the Salome legend, namely, the eroticizaton of the rapport between St. John and Salome, and her grotesque kissing and caressing of his bloody head. Although this variant seems nowhere present in literary texts antedating the nineteenth century, the subject of the forerunner's head served up on a platter and Salome's dance at Herod's banquet had often been depicted by painters as seductive. As his own volumes on the subject testify, Stendhal was well acquainted with Italian artistic masterpieces, and references to various "Herodiades" are scattered throughout his writings.

In France it is not until the second half of the nineteenth century that the erotic treatment of this legend begins to exercise its fascination in the artistic sector and on the literati. Zagona has traced its earliest manifestation to Heinrich Heine's *Atta Troll,* which appeared in 1841. Flaubert later dealt with the subject in his *Hérodias,* the last of the *Trois Contes,* in which the barely nubile body of Salome is offered to the reader thus:

> Sans fléchir ses genoux, en écartant les jambes, elle se courba si
> bien que son menton frôlait le plancher; et les nomades habitués
> à l'abstinence, les soldats de Rome experts en débauches, les
> avares publicains, les vieux prêtres aigris par les disputes, tous,
> dilatant leurs narines, palpitaient de convoitise.

The eroticization process gathered momentum with the presentation of Moreau's *L'Apparition* and *Salome* at the Spring Salon of 1876. In Moreau's mystico-byzantine rendition of the danseuse, Salome has emerged as an erotic femme fatale. Huysmans will then effect a point-by-point transliteration of this conception (and, in fact, of these two particular paintings) in his *A rebours* (1884), lending the scene a distinctly misogynist flavor, if indeed it does not inherently possess such overtones in the first place.

Mallarmé will transform the legend to his own literary ends in "Hérodiade," where the principle of chastity is treated with crystalline eroticism. However, it would take an Oscar Wilde to fetishize completely the Baptist's detached member. This author's glittering drama *Salome* was subsequently adapted by Strauss in his opera of the same name: legend had come full circle and dance was restored to itself. In Wilde's rendition, it is Salome's lust that results in John's beheading. The fact of his becoming sexually unfunctional (because dead) almost seems to incite her desire: "Ah! Thou wouldst not suffer me to kiss thy mouth, Iokannan. Well! I will kiss it now. I will bite it with my teeth as one bites a ripe fruit. Yes, I will kiss thy mouth, Iokannan." Herod, appaled, expostulates: "She is monstrous, thy daughter. I tell thee she is monstrous."

So is Mathilde de La Mole's desire deemed monstrous ("affreuse volupté"); perhaps it partakes of the same monstrosity as killing one's father and sleeping with one's mother. To be judged monstrous is to be witnessed, as it were, *in flagrante delicto*. Fouqué observes as the demented Mathilde ("folie" having so often been applied to her case that it is difficult not to literalize it here) at last reenacts her hereditary narrative:

> Elle avait le regard et les yeux égarés. —Je veux le voir, lui dit-elle. Fouqué n'eut pas le courage de parler ni de se lever. Il lui montra du doigt un grand manteau bleu sur le plancher. . . .
>
> Elle se jeta à genoux. . . . Ses mains tremblantes ouvrirent le manteau. Fouqué détourna les yeux. . . . Lorsque Fouqué eut la force de la regarder, elle avait placé sur une petite table de marbre, devant elle, la tête de Julien, et la baisait au front.

Earlier, while contemplating Julien Sorel's lost prospects, Mathilde had indulged in an onanistic fantasy of this (once-and-) future decollation:

> Au milieu des *transports* les plus vifs, quand elle serrait contre son coeur la *tête de Julien: Quoi! se disait-elle avec horreur,* cette tête charmante serait destinée à tomber. . . . Les souvenirs de ces moments d'héroïsme et *d'affreuse volupté* l'attachaient d'une étreinte invincible (my emphasis).

It is difficult to see how (or indeed why) in the light of such graphic description, Imbert could advance the notion that the existence of Mathilde's forebear, Marguerite de Navarre, suffices to "poeticize" the deed. It is as if such acts called out for euphemization, as if, with Fouqué, one's gaze had to be averted. But instead of "poetry" the reader meets with horrible pleasure and frightful sensuousness. These sadistic oxymora crown that object which is the point of coalescence in *Le Rouge et le noir:* the dislocated head of Julien Sorel. The multiple narrative systems elaborated in the novel, be they framed or framing texts, reinforce each other, converging with all the more force on this most magnetic head. This, the text's ultimate convergence, its nexus, is, paradoxically, a rupture.

NARRATOLOGICAL OVERDETERMINATION

When Castex remarks of Julien Sorel that "il pouvait être le héro de plusieurs romans différents, selon que l'écrivain eût voulu développer telle ou telle de ses virtualités," he has hit very close to the mark. Nonetheless, the formulation of this insight signals the extent to which a narratological approach diverges from a character perspective. Castex is interested in elucidating the novel's plot in terms of the character Julien. That is, Julien is *so* complex that the plot devolving from him might have taken several directions. But the converse might just as well be maintained: as a persona, Julien is complicated precisely because he is the juncture of several combined fables—and his head defines the very locus of narrative overdetermination. In this light it becomes possible to appreciate *Le Rouge et le noir* as a masterpiece as formidable for its liberal appropriation of buttress-texts as for their subsequent dismissal.

If I have dwelt extensively on St. John, it is because Mathilde's ending was too seductive to resist. How to explain this conclusion so imbued with fin-de-siècle luster? Mathilde's novel and Julien's demise constitute a sort of premature construct, the prefiguration of a peculiar treatment of the Salome legend, which would only begin to surface thirty years after the composition of *Le Rouge et le noir* and was to be fully articulated only some sixty years later. Still, the most that can legitimately be claimed—for here we strike the limits of intertextual approaches—is that this "realist" novel perhaps has the status of a prototype, and this possiblity has gone virtually unrecognized.

For the purposes of a narratological viewing of *Le Rouge* which proposes to devote particular attention to the problematic ending, the reinforcement of Mathilde's novel with a proto-narrative can only seal the conviction that the true conclusion of this novel lies somewhere beyond the decapitation. Now, there may well be some level at which this "belated" conclusion is experienced merely as narrative residue: this recalls Prévost's remark that at the end "l'élan que son imagination [Stendhal's] prenait pour un livre n'était pas épuisé à la dernière page . . . ," but, when one takes into consideration Marguerite de Navarre's drama in its atavistic reenactment by Mathilde and Salome's virtual plot lying beneath it all, the parts of the puzzle revolving around the burial of Julien Sorel fall into place; so much so, indeed, that the "signifying end" shifts from the hero's decollation to his interment. Thus, in a narratological sense the extended ending is triply determined. This, however, constitutes a necessary, but insufficient condition of meaning. For, if the structures set forth are formally complete, they remain to be vested with their psychological content.

THE INCANTATORY POWERS OF THE NAME OF THE SON

Just as it has been necessary to shed *Le Rouge et le noir* in order to arrive at the novel's original title, *Julien,* we see at last how essential it was that Julien free himself of the patronym: because it is the name of the son which mediates the various levels of the narrative grid, giving access to filial plots at other depths. Julien Sorel is eponymously linked to Julianus (with Napoleon interposed), whose life implicated the death of John the Baptist, itself indissociably attached to the story of Salome. Hence the onomastics of paternalism once shunted aside, the reader finds him/herself confronting the narrative matrix.

In *S/Z* Barthes reached similar conclusions as to the power of the name. Although his conception of character is moulded essentially on a grammatical model, and his terms of expression are syntactic, the points of similarity make it pertinent here:

> Ainsi, d'un point de vue classique (plus psychologique que symbolique), Sarrasine est la somme . . . de: *"turbulence, don artistique, indépendance, violence, excès, féminité, laideur, nature composite, impiété, goût du déchiquetage, volonté,"* etc. Ce qui donne l'illusion que la somme est supplémentée d'un reste précieux (quelque chose comme *l'individualité,* en ce que, qualitative, ineffable, elle échapperait à la vulgaire comptabilité des caractères composants), c'est le Nom Propre, la différence remplie de son *propre.* Le nom propre permet à la personne d'exister en dehors des sèmes, dont cependant la somme la constitue entièrement. Dès lors qu'il exite un Nom . . . vers quoi affluer et sur quoi se fixer, les sèmes deviennent des prédicats, inducteurs de vérité, et le Nom devient sujet.

Now, while Barthes situates character in the field of sememes and is, thus, dealing with irreducible units, here I am expanding his model by making story line the basic unit of composition. Julien Sorel's plot is the manifest etching on a palimpsest of narratives. And his name functions as a corridor of access, mediating the layers of plot, synthesizing them, binding them together as metaphor amidst the multiple texts' metonymic courses.

And perhaps for Stendhal a conception of narrative as grid was one way of halting or limiting time, in the same way that Rome was described by him not sequentially, but topographically. What I hope to show in the final chapters of this study is that *Le Rouge et le noir* tends towards the overwhelming of the temporal by space and the circumscribing of history by myth and the "real" by fiction.

Chronology

1783	Henri Beyle is born in Grenoble to Cherubin-Joseph Beyle and Caroline Adélaide Gagnon.
1790	Beyle's mother dies, leaving him to pass an unhappy childhood with his father, whom he hates bitterly.
1799	He completes his studies at the Ecole centrale de Grenoble and wins the school's first prize in mathematics. He leaves for Paris and arrives the day after the 18 Brumaire, when Napoléon Bonaparte staged the *coup d'état* that ended the French Republic.
1800	Beyle serves in Milan as a second lieutenant. Meets Angela Pietragrua.
1801–2	He returns to Paris and resigns from the army.
1808–9	Beyle is named Intendant of Imperial Domains in Brunswick. His duties take him to Vienna and Hungary.
1810	Returns to Paris. Is named auditor to the Council of State and enjoys the honors and social status associated with his position as a higher civil servant in Napoléon's government.
1811	Takes a leave of absence and travels to Milan. Angelina Pietragrua becomes his mistress. He begins work on *A History of Painting in Italy*.
1812–13	Participates in Napoléon's Russian campaign.
1814	Leaves for Milan after the fall of Napoléon.
1815	Publishes *The Lives of Haydn, Mozart, and Metastasio*.
1817	Uses for the first time the pseudonym "Stendhal." Publishes *The History of Painting in Italy* and *Rome, Naples, and Florence*.
1818	Falls in love with Mathilde Viscontini Dembowski, who rejects him.
1821	Stendhal resides in Paris, and participates actively in the intellectual life of the times.

1822   Publishes *On Love*.

1823   Publishes the first part of *Racine and Shakespeare* and *Life of Rossini*.

1827   Stendhal begins to write the series of short stories that were to be published posthumously as the *Italian Chronicles*. Publishes *Armance*.

1829   Begins to write *The Red and the Black*.

1830   Stendhal observes the July Revolution from his window as he corrects proofs of *The Red and the Black*, which is published later that year. He is appointed French Consul to Trieste by Louis-Philippe.

1831   Appointed consul at Civitavecchia.

1832   Stendhal writes *Souvenirs d'égotisme*.

1834–5   Starts to write *Lucien Leuwen* and *The Life of Henry Brulard*. Neither work will be finished at the time of his death.

1837   Back in Paris, Stendhal starts to write *Mémoires sur Napoléon,* and publishes a few more of the *Italian Chronicles*.

1839   Publication of *The Charterhouse of Parma*. Starts to write *Lamiel*. Returns to Italy.

1840   Revises *The Charterhouse of Parma* in response to the suggestions made by Balzac in his favorable review of the novel.

1841   Stendhal suffers his first stroke and returns to Paris.

1842   Continues work on the *Italian Chronicles*. Suffers his second and final stroke, and dies soon after on March 23.

Contributors

HAROLD BLOOM, Sterling Professor of the Humanities at Yale University, is the author of *The Anxiety of Influence, Poetry and Repression,* and many other volumes of literary criticism. His forthcoming study, *Freud: Transference and Authority,* attempts a full-scale reading of all of Freud's major writings. A MacArthur Prize Fellow, he is the general editor of five series of literary criticism published by Chelsea House. During 1987–88, he served as Charles Eliot Norton Professor of Poetry at Harvard University.

RENÉ GIRARD is the Andrew B. Harmmond Professor of French Language and Literature at Stanford University. His essay on *The Red and the Black* in this collection was taken from his important book, *Deceit, Desire and the Novel.* Other works of Girard available in English include *Violence and the Sacred* and *To Double Business Bound.*

HARRY LEVIN is Irving Babbitt Professor of Comparative Literature, Emeritus at Harvard University. His books include *The Question of Hamlet, The Gates of Horn, The Overreacher: A Study of Christopher Marlowe,* and *Shakespeare and the Revolution of the Times.*

D. A. MILLER has also written on the novels of George Eliot, Jane Austen, and Balzac. He teaches in the English Department of the University of California at Berkeley.

PETER BROOKS is Tripp Professor of the Humanities at Yale University. He is the author of *Reading for the Plot, The Melodramatic Imagination,* and *The Novel of Worldliness.*

ANN JEFFERSON is a research fellow in French at St. John's College, Oxford. She is the author of *The Nouveau Roman and the Poetics of Fiction* and is the editor, with David Robey, of *Modern Literary Theory: A Comparative Introduction.*

Margaret Mauldon is a member of the Five College Associates Program in Amherst, Massachusetts. Her specialty is the French epistolary novel and its public.

Carol A. Mossman is Assistant Professor of French at the University of Maryland, College Park. She is the author of *The Narrative Matrix: Stendhal's* Le Rouge et le noir.

Bibliography

Adams, Robert M. *Stendhal: Notes on a Novelist.* New York: Noonday Press, 1959.

Alter, Robert, and Carol Cosman. *A Lion for Love: A Critical Biography* of Stendhal. New York: Basic, 1979.

André, Robert. *Ecriture et pulsions dans le roman stendhalien.* Paris: Klincksieck, 1977.

Atherton, John. *Stendhal.* London: Bowes & Bowes, 1965.

Auerbach, Erich. "In the Hôtel de la Mole." In *Mimesis: The Representation of Reality in Western Literature,* translated by Willard Trask, 400–434. New York: Doubleday Anchor, 1957.

Bart, B[enjamin]. F. "Hypercreativity in Stendhal and Balzac." *Nineteenth-Century French Studies* 3, nos. 1–2 (1974–75): 18–39.

Blin, Georges. *Stendhal et les problèmes du roman.* Paris: Corti, 1954.

————. *Stendhal et les problèmes de la personnalité.* Paris: Corti, 1958.

Brombert, Victor. *Stendhal et la voie oblique.* Paris: Presses Universitaires de France, 1954.

————. ed. *Stendhal: A Collection of Critical Essays.* Englewood Cliffs, N.J.: Prentice-Hall, 1962.

————. *Stendhal: Fiction and the Themes of Freedom.* New York: Random House, 1968.

————. "Stendhal: The Happy Prison." In *The Romantic Prison: The French Tradition,* 62–87. Princeton: Princeton University Press, 1969.

Bulgin, Katheleen. "Love, Self-Esteem, and Narrative Perspective in Stendhal's *Le Rouge et le noir.*" *Essays in Literature* [Western Illinois University] 10, no. 1 (1983): 101–10.

Buss, Robin. "Quick on the Draw? Stendhal's Lottery Ticket and Some Early Critics of *Le Rouge et le noir.*" *Literature and History* 8, no. 1 (1982): 95–107.

Davidson, Joan Marie. "The Heroines in the Novels of Stendhal." *Centerpoint* 2, no. 2 (1977): 56–62.

DeLutni, Joseph R. "On an Episode of *Le Rouge et le noir:* 'L'Ennui'." *Nineteenth-Century French Studies* 3 (1975): 192–99.

Denomme, Robert T. "Julien Sorel and the Modern Conscience." *Western Humanities Review* 21 (1967): 227–34.

Felman, Shoshana. *La Folie dans l'oeuvre romanesque de Stendhal.* Paris: Corti, 1971.

Fowlie, Wallace. *Stendhal.* London: Macmillan, 1969.

Godfrey, Gary M. "Julien Sorel: Soldier in Blue." *Modern Language Quarterly* 37 (1976): 339–48.

Gutwirth, Marcel. *"Le Rouge et le noir* as Comedy." *Romanic Review* 56 (1965): 188–94.

Hemmings, F. W. J. *Stendhal: A Study of His Novels.* Oxford: Clarendon, 1964.

Jones, Grahame C. "The Dramatic Tempo of *Le Rouge et le noir." Essays on French Literature* (University of Western Australia) 6 (1969): 74–80.

Krutch, Joseph Wood. "Stendhal." In *Five Masters: A Study in the Mutations of the Novel,* 177–249. Bloomington: Indiana University Press, 1959.

Levin, Harry. "Stendhal." In *The Gates of Horn,* 84–148. New York: Oxford University Press, 1963.

Martineau, Henri. *L'Oeuvre de Stendhal: Histoire de ses livres et de sa pensée.* Paris: Albin Michel, 1951.

————. *Le Coeur de Stendhal.* 2 vols. Paris: Albin Michel, 1952–53.

May, Gita. "Stendhal and the Age of Ideas." In *Literature and History in the Age of Ideas,* edited by Charles G. S. Williams, 343–57. Columbus: Ohio State University Press, 1975.

Mossman, Carol A. *The Narrative Matrix: Stendhal's* Le Rouge et le noir. Lexington, Ky.: French Forum Publishers, 1984.

O'Connor, Frank. "Stendhal: The Flight from Reality." In *The Mirror in the Roadway,* 42–57. New York: Knopf, 1956.

Pollard, Patrick. "Color Symbolism in *Le Rouge et le noir." Modern Language Review* 76, no. 26 (1981): 323–31.

Prevost, Jean. *La Création chez Stendhal.* Paris: Mercure de France, 1951.

Proust, Marcel. "Notes sur Stendhal." In *Contre Sainte-Beuve,* 413–16. Paris: Gallimard, 1959.

Ragland-Sullivan, Mary Eloise. "Julien's Quest for 'Self': *Qui suis-je?" Nineteenth-Century French Studies* 8 nos. 1–2 (1979–80): 1–13.

Richard, Jean-Pierre. "Connaissance et tendresse chez Stendhal." In *Littérature et sensation,* 17–116. Paris: Editions du Seuil, 1954.

Richardson, Joanna. *Stendhal.* New York: Coward, McCann & Geoghegan, 1974.

Sands, Steven. "The Narcissism of Stendhal and Julien Sorel." *Studies in Romanticism* 14 (1975): 337–63

Starobinski, Jean. "Stendhal pseudonyme." In *L'Oeil vivant,* 191–244. Paris: Gallimard, 1961.

Strachey, Lytton. "Henri Beyle." In *Books and Characters French and English,* 267–93. New York: Harcourt, Brace, 1922.

Strickland, Geoffrey. *Stendhal: The Education of a Novelist.* Cambridge: Cambridge University Press, 1974.

Tillet, Margaret. *Stendhal: The Background to the Novels.* London: Oxford University Press, 1971.

Turnell, Martin. "Stendhal." In *The Novel in France,* 127–216. New York: Vintage Books, 1958.

Wood, Michael. *Stendhal.* Ithaca, N.Y.: Cornell University Press, 1971.

Yalom, Marilyn K. "Triangles and Prisons: A Psychological Study of Stendhalian Love." *Hartford Studies in Literature* 8 (1976): 82–97.

Acknowledgments

"*The Red and the Black*: Deceit and Desire" (originally entitled "*The Red and the Black*") by René Girard from *Deceit, Desire and the Novel*, translated by Yvonne Freccero, © 1965 by the Johns Hopkins University Press, Baltimore/London. Reprinted by permission of the Johns Hopkins University Press.

"*The Red and the Black*: Social Originality" (orginally entitled "The Happy Few") by Harry Levin from *The Gates of Horn* by Harry Levin, © 1963 by Harry Levin. Reprinted by permission.

"Narrative 'Uncontrol' in Stendhal" by D. A. Miller from *Narrative and Its Discontents* by D. A. Miller, © 1981 by Princeton University Press. Reprinted by permission of Princeton University Press.

"The Novel and the Guillotine, or Fathers and Sons in *Le Rouge et le noir*" by Peter Brooks from *Reading for the Plot: Design and Intention in Narrative* by Peter Brooks, © 1984 by Peter Brooks. Reprinted by permission of the author and Alfred A. Knopf, Inc.

"Stendhal and the Uses of Reading: *Le Rouge et le noir*" by Ann Jefferson from *French Studies* 37, no. 2 (April 1983), © 1983 by the Society for French Studies. Reprinted by permission.

"Generic Survival: *Le Rouge et le noir* and the Epistolary Tradition" by Margaret Mauldon from *French Studies* 38, no. 4 (October 1984), © 1984 by the Society for French Studies. Reprinted by permission.

"What's in a Name: Ur-texts, *Hors-texte*, Intertexts" by Carol A. Mossman from *The Narrative Matrix: Stendhal's* Le Rouge et le noir © 1984 by French Forum Publishers, Inc. Reprinted by permission.

Index